had a
glass

had a glass

TOP 100 WINES FOR 2008
UNDER $20

Kenji Hodgson | James Nevison

whitecap

Edited by Ben D'Andrea
Cover design and icons by Five Seventeen
Interior design and illustrations by Jacqui Thomas
Typeset by Jesse Marchand
Photo editing by Mark MacDonald
Photography by Michelle Mayne, James Nevison, and Kenji Hodgson

LIBRARY AND ARCHIVES CANADA CATALOGUING IN PUBLICATION

Hodgson, Kenji

Had a glass : top 100 wines for 2008 under $20 / Kenji Hodgson, James Nevison.

ISBN 978-1-55285-898-1
ISBN 1-55285-898-7

1. Wine and wine making--Canada. I. Nevison, James II. Title.

TP548.H628 2007   641.2'20971   C2007-901704-5

The publisher acknowledges the financial support of the Government of Canada through the Book Publishing Industry Development Program (BPIDP) and the Province of British Columbia through the Book Publishing Tax Credit.

Printed and bound in Canada by Friesens.

contents

7 **Preface—The Juice**

7   • Balance Is Big

7   • Organic Wine

8   • White Is the New Red?

9   • Getting On with It

11 **A Brief Guide to Wine Enjoyment**

12   • Had a Glass?

12   • Buyer Beware

13   • The Value Proposition

14 **How to Taste Wine**

15   • The Four Steps

16   • Taking Notes

17   • Usual Aromas

17   • Unusual Aromas

17   • Flights of Fancy

19   • Self-Help for Wine Monotony

20 **How to Buy Wine**

21   • Get Organized

23   • Occasional Wine

25   • Feelings, Nothing More Than Feelings

26   • Required Reading: Decoding a Wine Label

28   **How to Enjoy Wine**

29   · Glasses and Stemware

29   · Decanters

30   · Corkscrews

30   · Storing and Aging Your Wine

31   · Wine Handling

33   **Food and Wine**

34   · Strategies

36   · Icons

39   **Wine-Inspired Dishes, Mimi Approved**

40   · Mussels in White Wine

41   · Coq au Vin

43   · Marsala Prawns

44   · Sparkling Wine Jell-O

45   **The Whites**

82   **The Pinks**

86   **The Reds**

137   **The Bubblies**

143   **The Aperitifs**

146   **The Desserts**

151   **The Indices**

152   · Wines by Country

154   · Wines by Type

156   · Wines by Food

159   **Acknowledgements**

preface—the juice

Had a Glass 2008 focuses on real wine, that is, real good wine. Wine your mother-in-law will like. Wine to buy by the case. Wine that begins tasty and ends even tastier. More than ever before, wine styles are diversifying in the under-$20 category. This means plenty of opportunity to be picky about what you drink.

While choosing the top 100 for *Had a Glass*, we do our best to keep our noses out of our wine glasses. Sure, wading through the jungle of wines means locking ourselves in a room with hundreds of bottles, a couple of corkscrews, and a very large spittoon. But we eventually emerge—baring purple-stained teeth—to get on with finding out what matters more than fruit concentration and tannin structure.

That is, what kind of wines people want to drink.

Balance Is Big

2008 is all about balance. The more people we talk to—and share a glass with—the more we hear the call for wines that aren't going to do a coup d'état at the dinner table. It's less about the fruit bomb and more about the finesse. It's about wine that goes with food. Even more so, it's about wines that deliver the complete package. Whether they're white or red, light- or full-bodied, oaked or un-oaked, we're after wines with harmony.

Organic Wine

We're drinking organic like there's no tomorrow. A host of wineries are jumping on the green wagon, either turning a new leaf or starting to broadcast their organic philosophy.

For decades, the haphazard approach to organic wine set off oenophiles' alarm bells. In 2008, sustainable sipping doesn't mean compromising quality.

But when it comes to terminology, green is still grey. "Made from organically grown grapes" has become the accepted way to differentiate between organic farming and organic winemaking. The latter is rare, as great winemaking is nearly impossible without a few non-organic allowances.

However, indulging in a global selection of wine also means wading through a swath of differing legislation and certifying bodies, all with a unique definition of "organic." We're happy with the "made from organically grown grapes" slogan, but if you want to get technical, you could research endlessly to figure out each country's interpretation. If you're up for the task, we suggest that you at least have a glass of wine—from organic grapes, of course—on your desk.

Then there are those wineries that practise an organic philosophy but don't seek certification—and don't advertise on their wine labels. They might not meet all points for full certification, they might practise a toned-down version of organic, they might be in transition to organic, or they might just be concentrating on making great wine—and less on red tape. We might not be able to pick these off the shelf right away, but with a bit of investigation, it isn't hard to figure out who's into going green.

White Is the New Red?
We're happy to report a thirst-quenching number of amazing white wines in this 2008 edition of *Had a Glass*. Those sans skins stepped up to the palate in a big way. There's still nothing like a gargantuan glass of red to guzzle on a chilly evening, but when it comes to refreshment, easy sipping, the influx of Asian-influenced cuisine, and Saturday afternoons, nothing beats a chilled (or chill) glass of white wine.

White wine's popularity is rising. Red kept its sophistication factor for some years, but as wine quickly reaches peak popularity, the clichés are forgotten, and it's just as cool to drink white.

Labouring through the hundreds of wines for this book, we found many a complex, endearing white wine. From Gris to Grüner, there are some seriously superb white wines in this book.

Getting On with It
We're excited to present the *Had a Glass* picks for '08. We had a rollicking good time assembling one hundred drop-dead bottles. We hope you enjoy giving them a swirl.

Sip on,

Kenji & James

a brief guide to
wine enjoyment

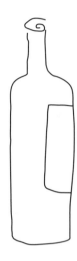

Had a Glass?

Had a Glass gives you the wine goods. In a veritable sea of vinous choice, *Had a Glass* points you in the right direction and makes sure you surface with a good bottle. And it won't cost you big money. The 100 wines in this book check in at under $20.

Each wine is here for a reason, whether it's perfect with a steak, ideal for a picnic, or simply a stand-alone sipper. And each one is a wine that we like to drink.

The wines come from a swath of countries and are made from a mix of grape varieties. They're reds and whites, sweets and dries. It's wine diversity we think you'll enjoy.

Pick a page, read the blurb, get the wine, and see what you think. Repeat often.

But remember: Quaffing the grape juice is tons of fun as long as you wine in moderation. Know your limit and always have a designated driver. Such is the path to true wine appreciation.

Buyer Beware

In compiling this list, we've taken care to select wines that are widely available. We all deserve good wine, no matter where we are.

Every effort has been made to ensure prices and vintages were correct at the time of publication. That said, the vagaries of wine buying and copy deadlines conspire against us. The good buys sell out, and the hot wines are subject to price increases.

Use this book as a starting point for your wine-buying adventures. Great bottles are out there, and like all good hunts, the fun is in the search.

The Value Proposition

"Value" is a dirty word, and its utterance leads to trouble. Like scoring wine on a 100-point scale, its objective scaffolding tries to prop up a subjective framework. "Value" is at best squishy and hard to pin down. But whether you're after price rollbacks at Wal-Mart or one-of-a-kind designer pieces, true value occurs when returns exceed expectations.

Here's how value is applied in *Had a Glass*

Our bank accounts set the upper limit of our wine budget at $20. Sure, on occasion we may spend more, but overall we toe the 20 line. From our research, most of you feel the same. We all love getting a great $15 bottle of wine. But we love cracking into a tasty $10 bottle even more.

Had a Glass celebrates those wines that give you the best bottle for the buck: the $10 wines that seem like $15, the $15 bottles that stand out, the $20 wines that taste like more. We see wine as an everyday beverage—not as a luxury—an enjoyable accessory to good living.

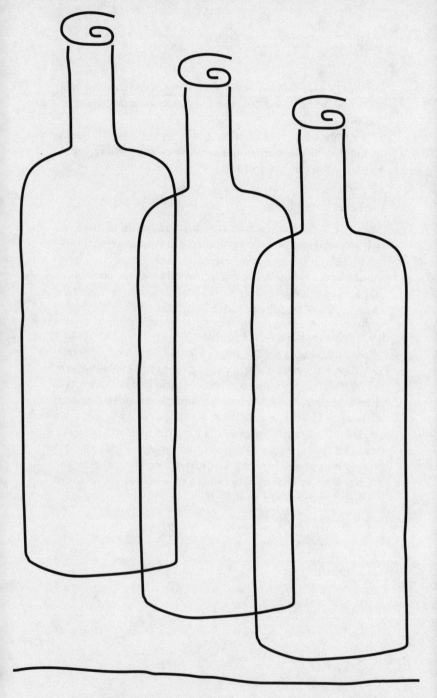

how to taste wine

Drinking wine and tasting wine are two different pastimes. If your only desire is to drink, by all means turn the page and get on to the reviews.

But, if you're ready to take your wine relationship to the next level, it's time to commit to proper tasting technique. It will add to your wine enjoyment as well as permit a complete sensory evaluation of the wine in your glass using taste, sight, smell, and feel.

We're tired of "A good wine is a wine you like." Sure, at the end of the day, it's your opinion that matters, but what makes a wine good? After you understand how to taste wine you'll be equipped to make that call.

The Four Steps

Here's the wine-tasting process in four simple steps.

Step 1—The Look

Tilt the wine glass away from you and observe the colour against a white background. Whites can be pallid yellow to deep gold, and reds range from the rich crimson of velvet drapes to the neon of raspberry Kool-Aid. Young white wines may have the brilliant sheen of white gold, while older reds often have complex tones of browns superimposed on sombre claret. Whites are typically clear, nearly transparent, whereas a red may be slightly cloudy with sediment.

Step 2—The Swirl

Swirl the wine glass—either on the table or in the air—to draw out the wine's aromas. Let the wine paint the sides of the glass with long, smooth tears, or legs. Note that these indicate texture and viscosity, not necessarily quality.

Step 3—The Smell

Smelling is wine intimacy. A deep inhale will reveal what the wine's about. Don't be afraid to put your nose into the glass. A wine may have the aromas of fruit (melons, berries, cherries), of wood (vanilla or smoke), or of spice (pepper or clove). You may also get a whiff of less likely aromas, such as earth, diesel, and leather. Surprising, maybe, but this is what makes wine exciting.

Step 4—The Taste

Take a generous sip of wine. Swirl it in your mouth. The consistency may be thin like skim milk (light-bodied) or it may be thick like cream (full-bodied). Let your tongue taste the different elements of the wine: any sweetness from residual sugars, any tartness from acid, or any bitterness from alcohol. Tannins may dry your gums, making you pucker. Spitting is optional.

Taking Notes

Whether you carry a leather-bound wine journal or scribble on a paper napkin, take wine notes whenever you can. At the very least, jot the name of the wine and a thumbs-up or down. This will save you from repeating the phrase, "I had a great wine last night . . . I think it had a picture of something on the label."

We use a tasting sheet like this:

TASTING NOTES

TASTING DATE

	WINE 1	WINE 2	WINE 3
WINE NAME • Vintage • Region • Price			
COLOUR • Straw Gold • Claret Purple • Clarity			
SMELL • Fruity • Woody • Spicy • Floral • Earthy			
TASTE • Sweetness • Acidity • Bitterness			
FEEL • Body • Tannin • Finish			
CONCLUSION • Balance • Quality • Do I Like This Wine?			

Usual Aromas

We know that wine smells like wine, but what does wine smell like? There are infinite aromas in fermented grape juice, and everyone smells something different. Here are a few usual aromas to get you started:

Red Wine	White Wine
• Blackberry	• Apple
• Raspberry	• Pear
• Plum	• Peach
• Vanilla	• Grapefruit
• Earthy	• Honey

Unusual Aromas

And then there are the weird scents. This is where wine gets interesting. A healthy imagination when tasting wine is good.

- Peking duck
- Leather chaps
- Wet fur
- Socks
- Toilet bowl

Flights of Fancy

Becoming a good wine taster is all about tasting wines. The more wines you try, the better your frame of reference. A great way to build your database and bolster your tasting skills is to approach wine in "flights." Create a flight by lining up a few wines that share a common theme. Tasting these side by side is like taking three pairs of jeans into the changing room.

Here are a few wine flights to get you started.

Flight 1—Sumptuous Spain

If any one country has made a serious splash in our liquor stores this year, it's Spain. Everyone seems to be rocking the Iberian libations, the saviours of great taste and greater value. Much of Spain's charm comes from its spectacular diversity of wine styles. Traditionally, Rioja was the mainstay of the country's wine, but recently we've been seeing plenty of promise from other regions and varieties.

    A. Glorioso (page 119)

    B. Las Rocas (page 116)

    C. Mad Dogs and Englishmen (page 112)

Flight 2—Serious Sauvignon Blanc

Never have we seen such a strong showing from Sauvignon Blanc. Too often brushed into the shadows of Chardonnay, or trendy varieties like Viognier, S.B. rarely gets first billing, let alone a second swirl. But Bacchus must be smiling on Sauvignon because there are a bunch of beauties in these pages. Try sipping these three side by side for a proper study of Sauvignon.

    A. Lurton (page 52)

    B. Santa Rita (page 51)

    C. Villa Maria (page 73)

Flight 3—Big ass red

Sometimes you just want to drink a big ass red. No excuse necessary; once in a while it's nice to have a wine that drinks like a meal. A wine that tells you what to think. A wine that takes no prisoners. There are some powerhouses out there, even in sub-$20 land, so dig in and pack a toothbrush.

    A. Angus (page 133)

    B. Escudo Rojo (page 131)

    C. Saxenburg (page 128)

Self-Help for Wine Monotony

If your wining has been monotonous of late, try these wine-buying strategies and never be stuck on the same bottle again.

Branching out

If you've been seduced by that special grape—like Malbec, a very seductive cultivar—then we'd wager you'll be just as taken with the same variety made elsewhere. No infidelity here, just wine diversity.

Malbec got famous in France, but these days, we see more celebrity Malbec from Argentina. Starting at the source, the Croix du Mayne (page 130) is a delicious introduction to Malbec. You'll get a taste of what the grape is all about in the Old World. Next, crack a bottle of the Argentine Pascual Toso (page 101) and Bodega Del Fin Del Mundo (page 99) to sample Malbec's modern home.

Love of the land

Certain parts of the world make certain types of wine. This is often denoted on the bottle by appellation, or where the wine originated. Names like "Côtes du Rhône" and "Chianti" are examples. If you like the wine of a particular app, try others from the same locale.

Both the Toscolo (page 121) and Ruffino's Il Ducale (page 132) hail from Tuscany, Italy, where some of the most pizza-friendly wines in the world are made. Both are superb examples of the enchanting wines that come from Tuscany's rolling hills.

Trading up

A winery commonly makes different tiers of wines—the Toyota and the Lexus. *Had a Glass* is all about the Toyotas, but if you like what you're test-driving, look for the luxury version.

The Spanish wine company, Torres, makes a broad range of very impressive wine. We love their Coronas (page 103) but across the board, from everyday affordable whites and reds (including the classic Sangre de Toro) to their top dog Gran Muralles, the wines are tasty.

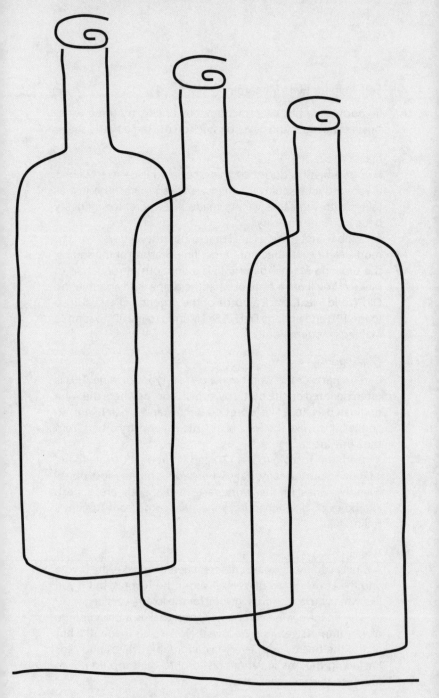

how to buy wine

Buying a bottle of wine shouldn't raise the heartbeat. Wine is fun, and strolling through your local bottle shop should be a joy. It isn't a visit to the dentist. But not everyone feels confident strutting through the liquor store like they own the joint, so we offer the following advice on how to buy wine.

Get Organized

The typical liquor store or wine shop organizes wine by country, a helpful categorical tool if you're feeling regional, but somewhat awkward if you want a Merlot and have to run around comparing one geographical offering to another. Things can get particularly unruly if you head to an Old World section like France or Italy and are confronted with regional names emblazoned across the labels instead of grape types. Get to know where certain grapes come from, and you'll be sleuthing through the bottle aisles in no time.

GrapeWHAT

What the grape? Different grapes have different personalities. Here, in five words or so, are the typical characteristics of the most common grape varieties.

Grape	WHAT?
Whites	
Chardonnay	apple, dry, often oaked, omnipresent
Chenin Blanc	green apple, steely, good acidity
Gewürztraminer	rich but refreshing, spicy, tropical
Pinot Blanc	fresh, fruity, mild, drink young
Pinot Gris	versatile, aromatic, honey
Pinot Grigio	same grape but Italian-style and crisp
Riesling	dry to sweet, good acidity, racy
Sauvignon Blanc	gooseberry, grassy, crisp, light
Semillon	lean or luscious, tupperware, honey
Torrontés	fresh, light, dry, floral
Viognier	trendy, floral, soft but peppy

Grape	WHAT?
Reds	
Cabernet Franc	raspberry, bell pepper
Cabernet Sauvignon	king grape, tannic, full, ages well
Carmenère	herbaceous, dark fruit, unique
Gamay	cherry, medium weight
Grenache	strawberry, bit rustic, potent
Malbec	plum, powerful, tannin
Merlot	approachable, smooth, full, dark fruit
Pinotage	South Africa, berry, spice
Pinot Noir	cherry, forest floor, soft tannins
Sangiovese	cherry, earthy, good acidity
Shiraz	medium, peppery, powerful, lotsa fruit
Syrah	same grape but less fruit, more earth
Tempranillo	juicy or dense, cherry or blackberry
Zinfandel	strawberry pie, brambles, jammy

GrapeWHERE

You're in a wineshop, standing in front of the Italy section, but the label just isn't telling you anything. What happened to Chardonnay and Merlot? It's a long story, but in the meantime here's the lowdown on what goes into some wines named by place.

Grape	WHERE?
Whites	
Semillon, Sauvignon Blanc	Bordeaux, France
Chardonnay	Burgundy, France
Viognier, Roussanne, Marsanne, and others	Côtes du Rhône, France
Marsanne, Grenache Blanc, and others	Côtes du Tricastin, France
Chardonnay, Pinot Noir, Pinot Meunier	Champagne, France

Grape	WHERE?
Reds	
Cabernet Sauvignon, Merlot, Cab Franc	Bordeaux, France
Pinot Noir	Burgundy, France
Gamay	Beaujolais, France
Syrah, Grenache, and others	Côtes-du-Rhône, France
Gamay	Beaujolais, France
Malbec	Cahors, France
Carignan, Grenache	Fitou, France
Sangiovese	Chianti, Italy
Tempranillo, Garnacha	Rioja, Spain

Occasional Wine

Of course, regardless of how the wines are organized, we're often there to buy a wine for a certain occasion, be it to go with mom's meatloaf or to celebrate Jane's birthday. This is a logical way to buy wine, especially—excuse us—for the occasional wine drinker. It's the time-honoured question: Do you match the wine to the food or the food to the wine? The answer will impact your wine-buying decision.

GrapeWHEN

Matching wines to food is like accessorizing an outfit. You want everything to go together, but that doesn't mean you have to be obvious. And there are bonus points for creativity.

Grape	WHEN?
Whites	
Chardonnay	chicken, crab
Chenin Blanc	snapper, salad
Gewürztraminer	curry, Asian
Pinot Blanc	goat cheese, veggie soup
Pinot Gris	halibut, smoked salmon
Riesling	turkey, apple sauce
Sauvignon Blanc	shellfish, fish
Semillon	prawns, pork
Torrontés	aperitif, carrot soup
Viognier	grilled fish, ginger
Champagne	in the bath with mango and a friend
Reds	
Cabernet Franc	roast, goulash
Cabernet Sauvignon	steak, kebabs
Carmenère	alone, late at night
Gamay	nachos
Malbec	slow-grilled food, stuffed cabbage
Merlot	Camembert, mushrooms
Pinotage	pork, game
Pinot Noir	salmon, duck
Sangiovese	pizza, pasta
Shiraz	BBQ
Tempranillo	bacon, beef stir-fry
Zinfandel	nachos, teriyaki
Port	with a book

Feelings, Nothing More Than Feelings

There's nothing better than matching wines to mood, and often when we find ourselves staring at a wall of wine wondering what to put in the basket, a simple mood check serves to stimulate the purchase process. A bold evening often calls for an aggressive wine, just as a mellow affair requires an equally subdued bottle. Feeling adventurous? Experiment with a new, never-before-tasted wine. Looking for a little comfort? Head back to the tried-and-true.

FEELING	TRY	FROM
Bold/Aggressive	Shiraz	Australia/B.C.
Mellow/Chill	Pinot Noir	France/California
Sophisticated	Cabernet Blend	Chile
Edgy	Riesling	Germany/Australia
Ambivalent	Chardonnay	Anywhere

LIKE	TRY	FROM
Cabernet Sauvignon	Tempranillo	Spain
Shiraz	Côtes du Rhône	France
Merlot	Malbec	Argentina
Chardonnay	Pinot Gris	B.C.
Sauvignon Blanc	Soave	Italy

Required Reading: Decoding a Wine Label

What appears on the wine label counts. You can learn a lot about a wine before you buy. The trick is to know what's worth reading. Wine label literacy can go a long way to increasing wine enjoyment and decreasing buyer remorse.

Old World

New World

Wine or winery name

Back in the day, the name would be that of a chateau or domaine, or possibly it'd be a proprietary name that was used by a winemaking co-operative. While these are still out there, now brand names, animal species, and hip monikers are gracing wine bottles—all in an effort to help you remember what you drank.

Vintage

The year printed on the label is the year the grapes were grown. There are good years and bad years, usually determined by weather conditions. Should you care? In good grape-weather years there'll be more good wine, but off years don't necessarily mean bad wine. If the winemakers know what they're doing, their wines will overcome the less-than-perfect vintages. A vintage also tells you how old the wine is. Oldies aren't necessarily goodies, but many wines improve with cellar time (page 31).

We include the vintages for the wines we review. Where no vintage is listed, the wine is "non-vintage," meaning it's been made from a mix of years.

Alcohol

Generally expressed as "alcohol by volume" (ABV) this tells you how much wine you can taste before the line between "tasting" and "drinking" becomes blurred. Or blurry. As a rough guide, a higher alcohol content (14% is high, anything above 14.5% is really high) suggests a heftier, more intense wine. On the other end of the ABV spectrum, wines with less than 11% will often be off-dry (slightly sweet). High alcohol doesn't mean a better wine. Regardless of the number, if the wine avoids the grating bitterness of alcohol, then it's a well-balanced drop.

Appellation

Or, where the grapes came from. Old World wine, say from France, often gives you the appellation instead of the grape variety. You'll see something like "Bordeaux," which describes where the grapes originated, but because French laws state only certain grapes are authorized in certain areas, the appellation name also hints at what grapes made the wine.

Grape variety

You pick up a can of soup and it's mushroom or tomato. On a wine bottle it's the grape variety that defines the wine: Shiraz or Merlot or Chardonnay, to mention a few. These are your "single varietal" wines, as opposed to "blended" wines, the likes of Cabernet-Merlot and Semillon-Sauvignon Blanc. Keep in mind, single varietal wines are no better than blends and vice versa. It all comes down to good winemaking creating good-tasting wine. Trust your taste buds.

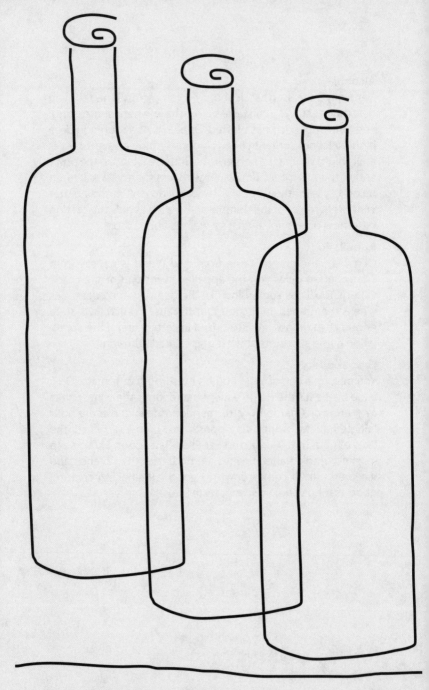

how to enjoy wine

Glasses and Stemware

Not all wine glasses are created equal, though drinking wine from any glass can be equally enjoyable. Allow us to explain.

Wine is like golf. There's an infinite array of specialized accessories, but all you really need to play the game is a set of clubs. Likewise, all your wine requires is a glass. It's up to you to decide how much you want to invest and how involved you want to get. Just don't tell us you can't drink wine because you don't have a wineglass.

There are benefits to good stemware:

- Swirling wine in the larger bowl common to fancy glasses does wonders for a wine's aromas. Pouring a few fingers at a time lets you get a proper swirl going.

- Holding the stem helps to keep white wines chilled and grubby fingerprints off the glass.

- There's no denying the elegant tactile sensation of a thin rim caressing the lips.

We use a motley collection of crystal we've collected over the years as well as a cupboard full of everyday tumblers for backyard bashes.

Decanters

After glasses, the next most important wine accessory is the decanter. A secret to wine enjoyment, the decanter can do more for your wines than you'd imagine. Decanting old red wines to remove the sediment from the liquid will keep your teeth clean, but how many of us drink old wines these days?

Use your decanter to decant young wines, letting them breathe. Most wines we buy are made to be drunk young—often too young—and decanting will open these wines up, revealing their character. Your decanter is a wine time machine; don't be afraid to shake it.

Anything can be used as a decanter, from a clean teapot to a water jug. To get serious about your decanter, look for a glass container with a wide base and a narrow opening. This facilitates swirling, makes for easier pouring—and looks pretty sexy.

Corkscrews

We've been to our share of dinner parties where the main event was getting the cork out of the bottle. Usually at the mercy of an antediluvian Butterfly corkscrew.

It would be a better wine world if everyone's knife drawer also had a Waiter's Friend. They're cheap (you can find them under $10) and effective (never yet met a cork it couldn't beat), and they make you look like you mean wine business when looped around your belt.

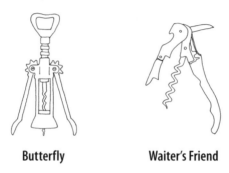

Butterfly   **Waiter's Friend**

Storing and Aging Your Wine

We don't mean to come across like we're down on wine cellars—quite the opposite. There's nothing we like better than rummaging around dusty wine racks sticky with cobwebs. But there's wine for aging and there's wine for drinking, and this book is about the latter.

In fact, over 90% of the wine sold today is made for drinking now, and to drink a wine now, you don't need a cellar. But, they say—and we've tasted proof—that wine changes as it gets older, hence the concept of storing wine.

Do you need a cellar or a sub-zero? For most, no. Display your wine in that IKEA wine rack, stash it in the cupboard, or keep it handy under your bed.

Wine Handling

Serving temperatures

18°C (65°F) *a bit below room temperature*	Red wine
10°C (50°F) *20 minutes out of the fridge*	White (and rosé) wine
5°C (40°F) *straight from the fridge*	Sparkling and sweet wine

Tips

- Err on the side of serving a wine too cold. The bottle will always warm up as it sits on the table.

- If you're not enjoying a wine, chill it well to mask many off-flavours.

- If a wine is too sweet, serve it cold to make it taste drier.

- All dessert wine should be served at fridge temperature, unless it's red—like port—in which case serve at the same temperature as red wine.

Leftovers

Once a bottle is open, how long do you have to drink it? Wine starts to deteriorate once it's exposed to oxygen, but finishing a bottle the following day—or if you must, even the day after—is fine.

Sure, there are tricks. Put the open bottle in the fridge, whether white or red, to slow down the oxidization, or use a vacuum pump to remove oxygen from the bottle, or buy spray bottles filled with inert gas to blanket the wine, protecting against oxygen, or drop marbles into the bottle to displace the air.

But if you ask us, you're better off breaking out a chunk of cheese and polishing off the contents.

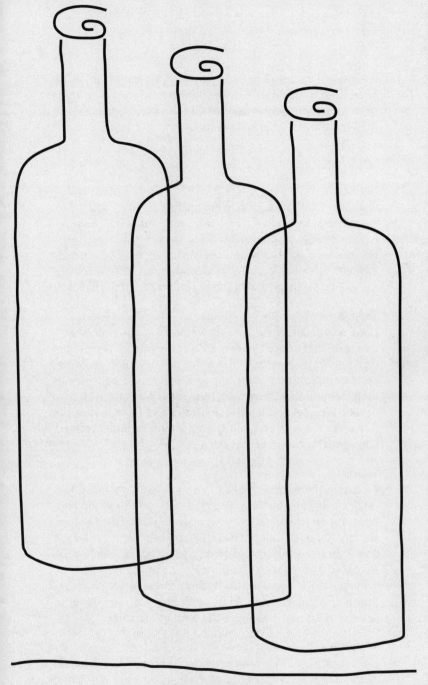

food and wine

We prepare our meals to match the wine we want to drink. We order a steak only if we feel like drinking red wine. But, we've been told, some people decide first what they're going to eat, then think about what wine to have.

Strategies

Red meat
Red wine. There are a lot of wine myths out there, and half of them are Grade "A" bull. "Red wine with red meat," however, is true. Besides synchronizing colours, red meat is hearty. It's full-flavoured and heavy, and red wines—especially Cabernets (page 133), Merlots (page 99), and Syrahs (page 93)—follow the same lines. **Strategy: match the big intensities of the flavours**.

Shellfish
Light, white wine. There are even white wines, like fino sherry, that taste briny. Could you ask for a better match? We also bet on white wines that have little, or no, oak flavour. These wines taste fresh, just how you want your shellfish to be. Rieslings (page 60) and Sauvignon Blancs (page 81) are tangy with crisp acidity. **Strategy: match the lightness and freshness of the flavours. Bonus strategy: if there's lemon or lime involved, wine with high acidity is good**.

Salmon
Medium white or lighter red wine. "Salmon steak" should tip you off. It's fish, sure, but if you've ever had spring salmon flopping around on the deck of your boat, you know the fish is no shrimp. Good B.C. salmon (wild, please) has plenty of flavour, and it takes a wine with extra heft to get along. White-wise, try oaked or un-oaked Chardonnays (page 71). Red-wise, try a Pinot Noir (page 114). And don't forget rosé (page 84). **Strategy: match a rich white with the rich omega-3s of salmon; if it's red, make sure the tannins are soft**.

White fish
Light to medium white wine. The way you cook the fish makes all the difference. Poached, go for a light wine like the Rudolf Müller (page 50) or the Heartland Stickleback (page 57). The delicacy of a poached fish needs a delicate wine. Baked, opt

for a bit of thickness from a white Côteaux du Tricastin (page 58) or a Pinot Grigio (page 64). Fried in a glorious sea of butter, open a Chardonnay (page 55). **Strategy: the more oil, the heavier your wine can be.**

Pork

Medium to full whites; light to medium reds. The "other" white meat can take to a lot of different wines. We love a good, off-dry Riesling (page 72) if there's a German flair to your cooking (read: apple sauce); we love a Spanish red (page 88) if it's pot roast. **Strategy: you can definitely put grapes before pigs. Pork is highly wine-friendly. It's all about how you sauce it.**

Chicken

Medium white wine. Everyone likes chicken, right? And everyone's happy with a medium-bodied, dry white wine. How can you go wrong? This is the perfect combo to serve the first time you cook for your date. Unless they're vegetarian. Then serve pasta alfredo. Unless they're vegan. Then serve tofu. Anyway, a Semillon blend (page 70) works, and if you want to get creative, try a Grüner Veltliner (page 79). **Strategy: hard to go wrong with white wine and chicken. Can work with cream sauce or tofu.**

Spicy

Fruity, off-dry white wine. Putting wine against spice is like pitting the "Dukes of Hazard" against the "A-Team." We pity the fool! In mild doses, a slightly sweet, fruity wine like Gewürztraminer (page 49) will show through spice, but if it's heavy jalapeño, go beer. Heavy red wines will upper-cut your palate and you'll taste nothing but hard-hitting tannins. **Strategy: get a white wine that has more flavour than the dish has spice.**

Heavy sauce

White or medium red. We learned the definition of "heavy sauce" in Paris. Cream and butter, baby. It challenges wine-pairing because whatever you put the sauce on tastes a lot like the sauce. If it's classic roux, a white like the Entre-Deux-Mers (page 69) or a soft, medium Pinot Noir (page 118) works. **Strategy: prevent cardiac arrest with some polyphenols and a walk around the block after dinner.**

Dessert
Red or white wine that's sweeter than the dessert. If the wine is too dry, the sweet dessert will make it seem even drier, and that's just way too dry for us. Both the "Clocktower" Tawny (page 150) and the Late Bottled Vintage Port (page 149) are sweet but not cloying, and this is why they rock. People seem to like dry red wine with chocolate. Here, make sure your red wine is full-flavoured and not too tannic, like The Black Chook (page 127). **Strategy: late harvest, icewine, port, sweet sherry, Madeira. This is your arsenal.**

Cheese
Try anything. It won't hurt. A wine salesperson once told us, "If you want to sell wine, serve cheese." The magical mud called cheese makes everything taste good. We highly recommend it before dinner, during dinner, and definitely after dinner. Creamy cheese is tasty with a creamy wine like the Wente (page 67), hard cheese with a solid wine like the Carm (page 126). A beautiful match is blue cheese and port (page 149). **Strategy: we always run out of cheese, so stock up.**

Icons

These icons will reappear in our list of top wines.

Food icons
Wine and food together is gastronomy in stereo. To help your pairings sing, here are some general guidelines:

 BEEF
Big protein: roast, steak, stew

 CHEESE
Hard or soft, stinky or mild

 CHOCOLATE
The darker the better

FISH
Trout, salmon,
halibut, tuna

LAMB
The other
red meat

ON ITS OWN

PORK
Chops, kebabs,
tenderloin

POULTRY
Turkey, chicken,
duck, guinea fowl

SHELLFISH
Bi-valves, oh my!
Oysters, mussels, clams

SPICY
Szechuan, mild curry,
Thai

VEGETARIAN
Tofu-friendly: stir-fries,
ratatouille, mushrooms galore

Occasion icons

 Wine is tied to experience. There's a wine for every occasion, but certain times call for specific wines. Whether the moment is casual or formal, serious or celebratory, a glass of wine can match the mood.

APERITIF
Suitable pre-meal to get the gastro-juices flowing

BEGINNER
Easy to drink, varietally true wines

BYO
Crowd-pleasers; wines to pack along

CELLAR
Wines that get better after a couple of years

PATIO/PICNIC
Hot weather sipping wines

ROCK OUT
Wines to let your hair down, tussle that do, and coif that mullet

ROMANCE
Wines to get busy with

WEDNESDAY WINE
To get you through the mid-week hump

WINE GEEK
Wines on the esoteric side that only a geek could love

WINTER WARMER
Wines to ward off any chill

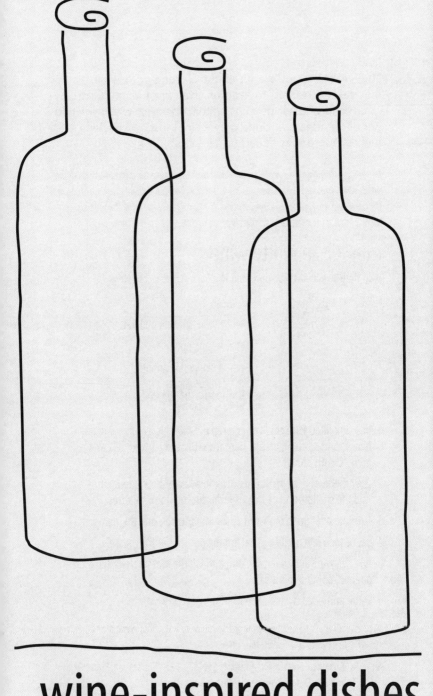

wine-inspired dishes
mimi approved

This year's recipes are all about cooking with wine! Sadly, schedules conspired to keep us away from Mimi, our trusty gourmand and recipe conspirator. However, when we told her of our idea to include only recipes inspired by wine, she replied, "More wine equals tastier food."

Mussels are surprisingly easy to prepare and cook and make for a quick yet satisfying meal. When it comes to bivalves, it's all about the broth, and there's no substitute for the tried-and-true white wine preparation. The key is to not overcook the mussels. Cook them just until the shells are completely open, and they'll be plump and juicy.

mussels in white wine

prep time 20 minutes | **cooking time** 10 minutes | **makes** 3 servings

2 lb (1 kg)	mussels
1 cup (250 mL)	white wine, dry and unoaked
2	shallots, chopped
2 Tbsp (30 mL)	butter, preferably unsalted
4–5 sprigs	fresh thyme (or 1 tsp/5 mL dried)

1 In a sink filled with cold water, prep the mussels by removing any beards and scraping off any barnacles. Discard any mussels that aren't tightly shut.

2 Over medium heat, melt the butter in a heavy-bottomed pot. Add the shallots and sauté until translucent, a few minutes.

3 Turn the heat up to high and add in the mussels and thyme.

4 Sauté for a few minutes, shaking the pot to coat the mussels.

5 Add the wine and cover, cooking until all the mussel shells have opened, about 5 minutes.

6 Serve immediately, ideally with a loaf of crusty bread.

note *Live mussels are tastiest during the cooler months. Remember the rule "any month with an R" for the juiciest morsels.*

serve 1. **Tarapaca Sauvignon Blanc (page 47)**, 2. **Villa Teresa Pinot Grigio (page 56)**, 3. **Wild Goose Riesling (page 63)**

Self-explanatory and simply revelatory when cooked with love, this classic French one-pot wonder is a perfect showcase for wine. Our version uses both red and white wine so you have half a bottle of each to serve alongside. Perfect match!

coq au vin

prep time 30 minutes | **cooking time** about 1½ hours | **makes** 4 servings

1	large chicken, or 8 thighs (see note below)
4 slices	bacon, cut into ½ inch thick pieces
1 Tbsp (15 mL)	butter
2	medium onions, chopped
2	carrots, coarsely chopped
2	celery sticks, coarsely chopped
2 Tbsp (30 mL)	flour
½ bottle (375 mL)	red wine (avoid heavily oaked wines)
½ bottle (375 mL)	white wine
4–5 sprigs	fresh thyme (or 1 tsp/5 mL dried)
2	bay leaves
12	pearl onions
10–12	white mushrooms, halved (about 200 g)

1 In a heavy-bottomed pot, melt the butter on medium heat and fry the bacon until it looks like Saturday morning breakfast. Remove to a large bowl.

2 In the same pan, add the chicken parts, skin side down, into the grease goodness. When the chicken has turned a pale golden, turn over and do the same for the opposite side. Remove to the bacon bowl.

3 In the even greasier goodness add the onions, carrots, and celery. Sauté the veggies, scraping up the sticky bits left over from the chicken. When the onions are translucent, add the mushrooms and sauté for another couple of minutes.

4 Put the chicken and bacon back into the pot, add the flour, and mix to coat.

5 Add the wine, the thyme, the bay leaves, and enough stock or water to cover the chicken.

6 Bring to a boil, then quickly turn down to a simmer.

7 Cover and simmer for 45 minutes.

8 Check the chicken. The meat should be separating from the bone. If not, leave in to cook for a bit longer. Remove the chicken to plates and keep warm.

9 Turn up the heat on the broth and let it reduce (no cover) until it starts to thicken.

10 Pour the reduced liquid and the veggies over the chicken.

11 Serve with roast potatoes or steamed rice.

note *It's best to use a whole chicken. Ask your butcher to cut it into 8 pieces for you. Or buy boneless thighs instead.*

serve 1. Chapoutier Coteaux du Tricastin "La Ciboise" (page 58), 2. Carmen Pinot Noir (page 104), 3. Torres Tempranillo "Coronas" (page 103)

The sweet richness of Marsala adds a whole new dimension to dishes. The Italians are experts at cooking with it, and every serious home chef should keep a bottle in the fridge at the ready. Prawns and mushrooms seem particularly suited to Marsala.

marsala prawns

prep time 30 minutes | **cooking time** 15 minutes | **makes** 4 servings

2 lb (1 kg)	large spot prawns, ideally live
3 Tbsp (45 mL)	extra virgin olive oil
1 rib	celery, sliced very thinly
1 medium	red onion, thinly sliced
4–5	plum tomatoes, coarsely chopped
2 Tbsp (30 mL)	capers, rinsed and chopped
¾ cup (175 mL)	Marsala
1	dried red chili, chopped
small handful	fresh basil, chopped (or 2 tsp/10 mL) dried
to taste	salt and pepper
optional	lemon wedge garnish

1 If using live shrimp, peel and devein.
2 Heat a heavy-bottomed pan on medium-high heat. Add the olive oil.
3 Add the celery, red onion, and chili; sauté until translucent, about 3 minutes.
4 Add the prawns and capers, season with salt and pepper, and toss to coat.
5 Cook the prawns until white throughout.
6 Add the Marsala and deglaze the pan.
7 Add the tomatoes and basil, and heat through.
8 Check the seasoning, adjust if necessary, and serve immediately.

serve 1. McWilliam's Riesling (page 61), **2.** Frescobaldi Pomino Bianco (page 77), **3.** Quails' Gate Rosé (page 85)

For anyone who loves Jell-O, here's a mature version of the shooters college students love. The sparkling wine fizz tickles the taste buds. Have fun creating your own fruit combinations.

sparkling wine jell-O

prep time 10 minutes | **cooking time** about 2 hours to set | **makes** 4–6 servings

1 box	powdered Jell-O mix
1 cup (250 mL)	water
1 cup (250 mL)	sparkling wine
½ cup (125 mL)	fresh fruit of your choice (except pineapple or kiwi)

1 Follow the directions on the Jell-O box, but replace the cold water with sparkling wine.

2 Add the chopped fruit for a touch of class.

3 Chill as per instructions.

4 Wibble and wobble to delight.

serve 1. Deinhard "Lila" (page 140), 2. Villa Maria Sauvignon Blanc (page 73), 3. Red Rooster Reserve Gewürztraminer (page 75)

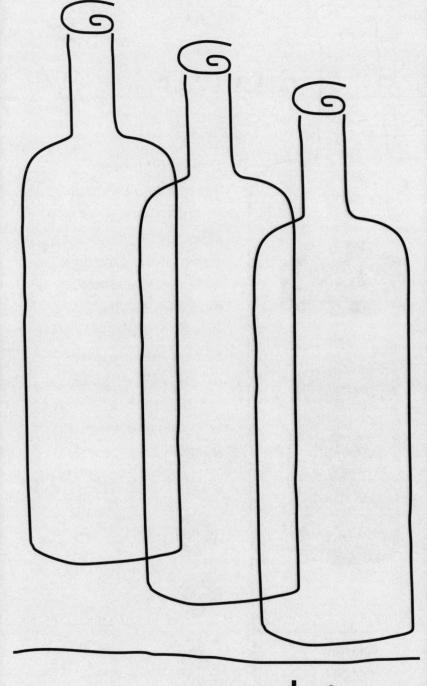

the whites

dunavar

**2005
Pinot Gris
$8.99**

Drum roll please . . .

Dunavar is the only wine to grace these pages three years running. We hemmed a bit, wondering if we'd let readers down by reviewing it again. But then we tasted the new vintage, noted the unbeatable price that's held fast, compared this Pinot Gris to the other sub-$10 wines on the shelf, and concluded that it would be a crime not to give Dunavar its due. Simply put, it's still the perfect white when buying by the case, which is what we'll be doing for weddings and office parties throughout the year.

 lasagna

 baked brie

 patio/picnic, Wednesday wine

Chile

tarapaca

Tarapaca's Sauvignon Blanc takes fresh to a new level, beyond any kind of fresh you're familiar with—fresh air, Freshjive, Fresh Prince. Grapefruit, lemon zest, and cut grass combine in this fearlessly affordable bottle that's perfect for any occasion, from patio gatherings to dance parties to, well, getting fresh.

 fish and chips

 chicken cacciatore

 beginner, patio/picnic

**2006
Sauvignon Blanc
$8.99**

gazela

Screw cap scandal?

Despite the seemingly frantic proliferation of the screw cap on quality bottles of wine, we never thought we'd see the tin top on something from Portugal. King of the cork, Portugal is home to the world's largest wine cork industry, and we did a double-take when we went to crack into the Gazela with a corkscrew only to find a black metal cap where the wood used to be. Politics aside, the Gazela is as good as ever (dare we say better?), with a massively appealing vivacity via tons of lime juice and a subtle fizz.

 on its own

 patio/picnic, aperitif

Vinho Verde
$9.99

cono sur

This is blogging wine.

You know, when it's 12:32 a.m. and you're sitting in front of your Mac with headphones on, listening to the new Blonde Redhead, or old Blonde Redhead, or maybe Avril Lavigne. Anyway, whichever way you punk (pop- or post-), while you blog away with raillery, sip on a bottle of wine. Not just any wine, but one that's packed with lychee, rose petals, and a full-on tropical explosion. Perfect for after hours in the blogosphere.

 on its own

 pad Thai

 aperitif, wine geek

**2006
Gewürztraminer
$10.99**

rudolf müller

**2004
RIESLING
CHARDONNAY**
Qualitätswein
PFALZ

**2004
Riesling/Chardonnay
$10.99**

You know the world is melding into one globalized shade of grey when wineries start mixing Riesling and Chardonnay. It's an atypical blend, bringing together two unlikely partners. But if Napolean Dynamite can envision a liger, then Rudolf Müller can bottle a Rieslonnay. We're glad they did, because this is one great-value white, showcasing Granny Smith apple, peach, melon, and mineral. A fine, food-friendly wine that will pair well with both fusion and classically prepared cuisine.

 spicy tofu

 basa tacos

 aperitif, Wednesday wine

Chile

santa rita

Since last year's edition, screw caps have propagated like blithe rabbits, or like hits on our website after we posted a picture of Tricia Helfer.
Bring on screw caps, we say, and bring on Tricia Helfer. Like everything, except weapons of mass destruction and Blind Melon, screw caps are good when used responsibly. This one seals in sexy aromas of grapefruit and peach.

 on its own

 quesadillas

 Wednesday wine, patio/picnic

**2006
Sauvignon Blanc
"120"
$11.99**

lurton

**2005
Sauvignon Blanc
"Les Fumées Blanches"
$11.99**

How do you know a wine is good? This question has stumped oenophiles for ages, prompting endless wine wrangling about acidity, tannin, body, phenolics … the list goes on. Numerical scales have been created to grade wine. Books have been written. The Internet proliferates the questions. Forget the soapbox spiel. Instead, crack open Lurton's Sauvignon Blanc. It's so infinitely tasty that you'll polish it off without even knowing it. Empty bottle = good wine.

 tempura

 trout with beurre blanc

 romance, patio/picnic

France

laroche

- **The wine snob.** Common in the jungles of the wine world, recognized by a disinterest in inexpensive bottles and non-crystal wine glasses. There's permanent open season on wine snobs, but they're costly to bait.
- **The wine geek.** Can be found among shelves with bottles from obscure European appellations. Often carries the 819-page *Oxford Companion to Wine*.
- **The *Had a Glass* pick.** Don't shoot, but buy. If it's this Laroche, buy a case. A gorgeous representation of Viognier, the wine smells like ginger root and tastes of peaches and apricots.

 roast quail with sage, chicken wings

 romance, wine geek

2005
Viognier
$12.99

adobe

**2005
Chardonnay
Emiliana Orgánico
$13.99**

Don't drink this because it's organic.

Drink the Adobe Chardonnay because it's a massively fruity, tropical bonanza. Punch bowl meets Super Lemon candies in a mash-up of pineapple juice, sweet-and-sour salvo—and booze. It's a sensory adventure. The smaller environmental footprint is a bonus reason to enjoy the Adobe; with flavour country like this, it's easy to be that conscientious connoisseur.

 casserole

 fried chicken

 Wednesday wine, beginner

Italy

mandrarossa

Wine personal: Thirsty palate looking for full-bodied, smooth Italian blonde. This estate-bottled beaut hails from the isle of Sicily—a ripe guava and pineapple Chardonnay that finishes with a creamy, spicy kiss.

 on its own

 oysters motoyaki

 beginner, BYO

2005 Chardonnay $13.99

villa teresa

**2006
Pinot Grigio
$14.95**

Organically grown grapes? Check. Traditional winemaking methods without using herbicides, pesticides, or chemical fertilization? Check. Clean label design, muted enough to match any table setting? Double check. Hip grape variety? At time of writing. Likeable price? Check again. What else do you need? This bottle passes the modern living test with flying colours, deemed fit for consumption as a well-rounded, consciously produced Pinot Grigio, showing pear and apple skin, anise, and a whiff of cheese in a great textured white.

 prawn tempura

 roast trout

 patio/picnic, BYO

Australia

heartland

The Stickleback is minimalist-maximalist in bottled form. Come to think of it, the über-cool label design would look right at home atop a Vernor Panton table. In this crisp white blend, the Chardonnay takes the back seat to the waxy lime and citrus bomb qualities of the other two grapes. In the end your palate is assaulted—in all the right ways—by an amazingly refreshing and zippy light white. Perhaps not the wine you'd swirl alongside a T-bone, but a fabulous example of the beauty in wine diversity.

 any kind of greasy chicken

 chili garlic pork chops

 aperitif, wine geek

**2005
"Stickleback White"
$14.99**

chapoutier

**2005
Côteaux du Tricastin
"La Ciboise"
$15.07**

***Fac et Spera* reads the
label.** Do and hope. Do the right
thing and try this tasty bottle. We can
hope that more $15 wines like this hit our
shelves. No stranger to the *Had* pages,
French vintner M. Chapoutier continues
to prove that you can make good wines
on a budget and with a conscience.
All Chapoutier wines are organic, and
the progressive producer continues to
embrace biodynamic farming at all his
vineyards. So, whether sipping on the
good value, mineral, and floral La Ciboise
or splurging on top-tier Hermitage, you're
getting wine made with care.

 suatéed prawns

 turkey pot pie

 Wednesday wine

Australia

penfolds

Australian wine has taken over the liquor store. We'll tell you this: lots of it is tasty, but just because there's more of it, doesn't mean it's all good. You still have to pick wisely, and we extend our heartfelt sympathy to anyone who's had a bad break (we wrote this book for you). To hedge your bets, go with this Koonunga Hill Chardonnay. First, it's a sublime concoction of pear and papaya, a smack of grapefruit, and a hint of toasty oak. Second, it has a lovely bright-red screw cap, guaranteeing the wine will always be pristine.

 pasta alfredo

 roast chicken

 beginner, patio/picnic

**2006
Chardonnay
"Koonunga Hill"
$15.07**

chateau ste. michelle

More proof that great Riesling can be grown worldwide. Here we go to Washington state for a drop so good it could stop traffic. Or was that just the Peace Arch crossing? Thankfully, we don't have to suffer in that much gridlock to get a taste of this peachy, pear-nectared, ginger-spiked elixir. Soft out of the gate, but finishes with freshness. This has "drink me" written all over it.

 crackling

 on its own

 BYO, patio/picnic

**2005
Riesling
$15.99**

Australia

mcwilliam's

The problem with wine bottles is they're never the right size. The lousy wines are always in bottles too big, and the good wines are never in bottles big enough. We'd like to see a towering behemoth bottle of McWilliam's Riesling on the dinner table, as it disappears far too quickly. It's fresh and zesty, with a lemon-lime bite and ripe-apple roundness—a delicious balance perfect for taking gigantic gulps.

 tofu hot pot

 steamed clams

 aperitif, BYO

**2005
Riesling
$15.99**

feudo arancio

**2006
Grillo
$15.99**

The Grillo grape needs a marketing campaign.

We thought it could use the J-E-L-L-O jingle, though it might run into a lawsuit when kids try to pack it in their lunch boxes. Perhaps the hip-hop route, with a "Grill-yo" dropped by Paul Wall or Neyo. Or maybe a "Grillo-yo" from Owen Wilson. The promo possibilities are endless for this southern Italian grape that's rarely tasted at Canadian tables. But don't wait for its appearance in *Zoolander 2*. Instead pick up a bottle of Feudo Arancio: apple peel, honey, and chopped walnuts.

 roast chicken

 squash soup

 patio/picnic, winter warmer

 British Columbia

wild goose

Wild Goose winery, tucked away near Okanagan Falls, has consistently produced exciting bottles. The trend continues with their latest Riesling, a peachy, mineral, honeyed little number that marries an off-dry, fruity mid-palate with an acidic bolt to finish. What more do you want? Solid. Turn the page for more wit.

 sweet and sour

 halibut with peach salsa

 patio/picnic, cellar

**2006
Riesling
$16.95**

mission hill

The Okanagan is a young wine region. Most of the valley's vines have been in the ground for only a handful of years as wine growing got serious only two decades ago. But a number of great, consistent, go-to bottles have emerged, and Mission Hill's Pinot Grigio ranks as one of them. The new 2006 vintage shows fine floral and peach aromas, followed by flavours of pear and apple, making for a delicious drop.

**2006
Pinot Grigio
"Five Vineyards"
$16.99**

 chicken strips with plum sauce

 grilled chops with applesauce

 aperitif, romance

inniskillin

It's famous in the Loire and prolific in South Africa, but when it comes to Chenin Blanc in this year's book, the irony is that the only one we found worth reporting is from the Okanagan. Under Inniskillin's fancy-label Discovery Series, we get treated to a grassy, honeyed, and powerful rendition of Chenin Blanc. As B.C. goes to the wall with some unique varieties, this bottle proves that local Chenin has charm.

 cheese ravioli

 gyoza

 wine cellar, geek

**2005
Chenin Blanc
"Discovery Series"
$16.99**

anakena

**2005
Viognier
$17.50**

We're not sure if we qualify to be in the "upwardly mobile" camp, but we're confident that this wine is yuppie-certified. It's a hot grape in a fashionable bottle; we envision urbanites strolling through Yaletown with a bottle of Anakena in the LV wine purse. Thankfully, at the price, you don't need to be DINK to give it a swirl, and the taste will satisfy all demographics. Not only is the label sleek and modern, the wine inside is a rich and sensual ginger root and rose petal perfume bomb that will leave your palate feeling sophisticated.

 salmon curry

 five-spice pork

 aperitif, BYO

California

wente

Vines can thrive in a lot of out-of-the-way places, but San Francisco Bay? From the Mission to Chinatown, there are some great eats, but so far, no downtown vineyards to speak of. In an odd bit of vinous trivia, "SF Bay" refers to grapes coming from 1.5 million acres stretching well beyond the city—though, curiously, it also encompasses the urban centre. Taste a little San Fran terroir in Wente's toasty, ripe apple, and sweet vanilla offering, complete with buckets of pineapple and butterscotch flavours for good measure.

 seafood pasta

 fried chicken

 BYO, beginner

**2005
Chardonnay
"Livermore Valley"
$17.99**

babich

2006
Sauvignon Blanc
"Marlborough"
$17.99

Admittedly, New Zealand Sauvignon Blancs are in danger of coming across like one-trick ponies. But this pony still has huge style. It's all here: textbook fresh lime fruit, jalapeño, intense gooseberry. This is the wine equivalent of bottled lightning. And yet just as it zings the palate it lifts the soul. It's softer than anticipated: fresh but lush, zesty yet richly elegant.

 Cajun

corn fritters

 romance, patio/picnic, rock out

France

lurton

Bonnet is 4:20 p.m. wine. This time of day calls for cracking the neon green screw cap on a bottle of Château Bonnet and inhaling the grassy, grapefruit, and lime rind aromas. No half-baked swill, this white Bordeaux (here a blend of Sauvignon Blanc and Semillon) is the freshest thing on the block, yet so under-appreciated. Delicious on its own. But just in case, we recommend some snacks at the ready.

 Morbier

 crackers

 aperitif, patio/picnic

**2005
Château Bonnet
Entre-Deux-Mers
$17.99**

grant burge

**2005
Semillon/Sauvignon Blanc
$17.99**

If there was a wine draft, we'd take Semillon and Sauvignon Blanc in the first round. Those Bordelais brains nailed a great combo when they put the two grapes together. Sauvignon Blanc brings a grassy, lemon/lime freshness to the team, while Semillon, like a good bullpen, adds depth. From Grant Burge we get a citrus fastball changed up by the Semillon's waxy, lanolin touch. No goopball, just great wine.

 stir-fried green beans

 winter warmer, patio/picnic

California

bonterra

Back in the day, wearing your organic bias on the label was a hindrance. Organic wines had a reputation as bad as those under screw caps. But now we're living in a wine revolution, with the benefits of both screw caps and organics being hailed far and wide, and we welcome the chance to choose quality that satisfies our green palates with apple butter and nicely integrated oak, and assuages our food-mile guilt with its spicy vanilla finish.

 chicken kebabs

 terrine

 beginner, BYO

**2005
Chardonnay
$17.99**

lingenfelder

**2005
Riesling
"Bird Label"
$18.05**

We could open a bird sanctuary what with all the quail, geese, and guinea fowl running around on the labels of the bottles in this year's book. We haven't the foggiest why so many wine labels feature fledglings. After all, birds are the arch enemies of a ripe vineyard. Maybe it's just a cute thing to put on a wine bottle. Certainly Lingenfelder led the charge with the eminent "Bird Label" Riesling. But let's get on with what's in the bottle. Crack this screw cap to reveal a gorgeous bouquet of lime rind, honey, lychee, and spice.

 hocks, schnitzel

 wine geek, cellar

New Zealand

villa maria

Who needs a spa treatment when you've got a bottle of Villa Maria?

This is the wine equivalent of the hot sweat/cold soak. We'd pick up a six-pack of this killer Sauv Blanc over spending an hour in the sauna any day. Both will leave you feeling refreshed, and with the five leftover bottles we'll be frequently wetting our whistles and nourishing our bodies. Its bracing citrus and gooseberry goodness will open the pores, while the rich, well-balanced texture will soothe the soul.

 grilled halibut

 sushi

 aperitif, Wednesday wine

**2006
Sauvignon Blanc
$18.99**

bollini

**2005
Pinot Grigio
$18.99**

Sometimes we don't know which end is up.

There was a time when "Pinot Grigio" meant Italian, light, fresh, and hopefully not insipid. "Pinot Gris" usually signaled New World—richer, rounder, and hopefully only a hint of funkiness. Same grape, yes, but diverse styles helpfully demarcated by nomenclature. Now Bollini sends us this rich and leesy, apple skin and pear core, lush Grigio. All we can do is throw up our hands and drink the winning result. This is what real Italian Pinot Grigio is all about.

 on its own

 chicken *sous-vide*

wine geek, BYO

red rooster

Too often we forget that wine comes from the vineyard, not from the winery. RR's Reserve Gewürztraminer has its origins in Summerland, from a picturesque vineyard owned by Peter Krieger, an amiable German with a really cool dirt bike. While standard bird-control practice is either loud bangs from a noise cannon or covering the vines with nets, Peter prefers to tear up and down the rows of vines on his bike, honking a noisy horn. But who are we to pass judgment on his hands-on approach? From his vineyard grew this aroma-bomb of a wine, packed to the brim with nuances of everything except the kitchen sink. Lychee, rose petal, spice, tropical notes, citrus tang—it's all in here.

 mild curries: Indian, Thai, or Glico

 romance, rock out

2006
Gewürztraminer
"Reserve"
$19.95

château de chasseloir

Welcome to a wine that you can sip all afternoon. We're not talking about a wine for lunch or a pre-dinner tipple. We're talking pop the cork on this bad boy and gargle it from high noon to sundown. Ultra-fresh aromas of lemon, lime, and mineral mesh with a unique creaminess to make for a wine that defies boredom. We always say, enjoy wine with a friend, but here we find ourselves breaking the rule. At a supremely drinkable 12% ABV, with this bottle you can go it alone.

**2005
Muscadet Sevre
et Maine Sur Lie
$19.95**

 antipasti

 oysters

aperitif, romance

Italy

frescobaldi

Frescobaldi's Pomino Bianco gives us goose bumps. Not because we chilled it in the fridge for too long, but because it's eerie how good a bottle of wine can be. Give it up for Chardonnay mixed with a little Pinot Blanc (or "Bianco" if you want to get Italian) making a deliciously fresh, yet full-flavoured, fermentation that exudes Anjou pears, clover honey, and a lip-smacking finish of Granny Smith apples. A whole orchard stuffed into a bottle of wine. Uncanny.

 tempura

 halibut cheeks

 rock out, patio/picnic

**2005
Pomino Bianco
$19.99**

leitz

LEITZ

2004
Rheingau
Riesling
Kabinett

RHEINGAU | GERMANY

R I E S L I N G

2004
Riesling
$19.99

Just to prove that you can never have too much Riesling, we've included one more.

Officially outnumbering Chardonnays, Semillons, and Poulsards (OK, we're still working on getting a Poulsard into *Had a Glass*), it seems there's plenty of great Rieslings out there waiting to be taken home and loved. Radical Rieslings. Rhinestone Rieslings. Rip-roaring Rieslings. The Leitz is all of this and more. Inhale the gorgeous lime rind, slate, and honey aromas; quaff the thick, lush baked apple and Florida grapefruit libation.

 choucroute garni

 chicken curry

 wine geek, cellar

Austria

schloss gobelsburg

We're concerned about Grüner Veltliner. Punters seem to be over the "GruVee" stage, so we're afraid this magnificent white will be another wine trend victim. The thing is, unlike neon and sweatpants, once in a while a bottle like this elegant, nougat, mineral, and white pepper nuanced Gobelsburger is unbeatable. Start with the occasions listed below, and let Grüner become part of your routine wine affair—rather than the next "it" white.

 chili salt crab

 fondue

 wine geek, cellar, patio/picnic

**2004
Grüner Veltliner
"Gobelsburger"
$19.99**

see ya later ranch

Long summer days call for Chardonnay.

More specifically, when the sun starts its descent in the west, bathing the world in toasty golden hues, it's time to break out a bottle like this SYL. A lush, full-bodied bombshell of apple blossom and tropical fruit backed by supple wood spice, this is liquid sunshine.

 shrimp cocktail

 on its own

 patio/picnic, BYO

**2005
Chardonnay
$19.99**

New Zealand

jackson

Sure, there are the conspiracy theories, like "grassy" Sauvignon Blanc is just unripe grapes. But we're not here to argue about any grassy knoll, and Kiwi SB is tasty—Jackson's delectable example proves it. Get ready for gorgeous gooseberry and honey aromas backed by lime wedges and guava. Yum.

 gyoza

 bouillabaisse

 aperitif, patio/picnic

**2006
Sauvignon Blanc
$19.99**

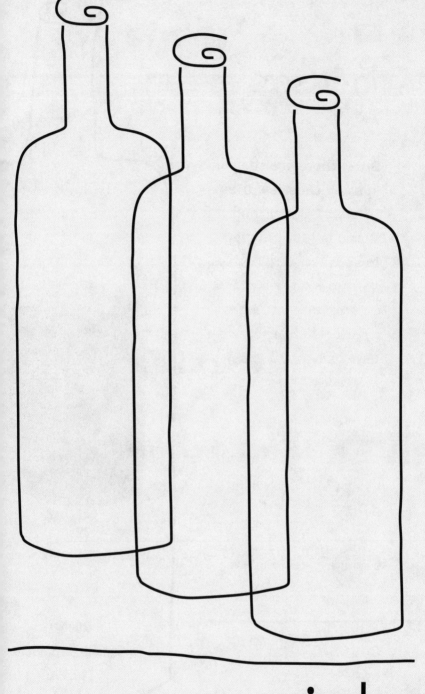

the pinks

viña chocalán

Bring on the great value rosé! Honestly speaking, rosé isn't one of those wines we want to go out and spend a boatload on. Pink wine is all about good times—save the hard-earned lucre for cellar reds and whites. The Chocalán crams a lot of rosé into the bottle for the price, with lots of cherry pie filling, some earthiness, and a big strawberry finish. The perfect sipper to accompany cards in the sunroom.

 roast quail

 schwarma

 patio/picnic, BYO, romance

**2006
Rosé Syrah/Petit Verdot
$12.99**

marqués de cáceres

Wake up and see the world through rose-coloured wine glasses.

Seriously, it's a trip. You need to borrow your friend's glass to have one for each eye, which makes you look pretty unsophisticated—but sod 'em. Then you swirl the glasses in front of your eyes and the world takes on this distorted, pink fantasyland appeal. Then you can try swirling each glass in opposite directions, which makes the world spin awkwardly, as if you'd consumed an entire bottle of this amazingly rich strawberry Spanish rosé.

 paella

 brie

 patio/picnic, wine geek

2006 Rosado $14.99

British Columbia

quails' gate

With every new vintage of *Had a Glass*, we work our palates to expand the rosé section. Such a crucial element to wine enjoyment—a segue between the white course and the red, an answer for the wine waffler, the all-star summer sipper—yet it's only gradually catching on. We still struggle to find a handful of radical rosés, but thankfully Quails' Gate's offers one of them. With loads of strawberries and rhubarb, this wine is all freshness and fun.

 seafood risotto

 on its own

 patio/picnic, BYO

2006
Rosé
$14.99

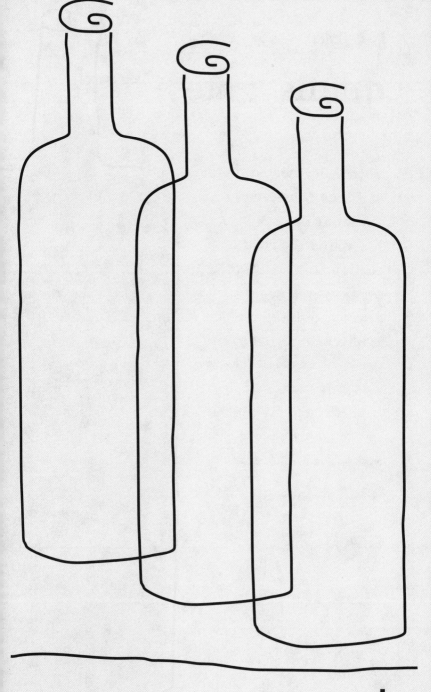

the reds

Italy

citra

File this wine under drinkable. This is the bottle you bring out at 10 p.m. in a symbolic gesture that says, "It's time to keep the party going." It's also the type of wine you put on the table mid-week to go with take out lasagna or pizza. It's simple, and simply fun to drink. Perfect in its role as social lubricant, just as wine was intended.

 pizza

 bocconcini

 Wednesday wine, rock out

**2005
Montepulciano D'Abruzzo
$9.49 (for 1 litre)**

bodegas piqueras

This wine is kinda trashy, and we mean that as the utmost compliment. It's just that this puts out so much for 10 bucks—juicy raspberry, brambly branches, cigarette butt—that it's almost a crime. Not only that, it has the nerve to be well-balanced and food-friendly, qualities often lacking in so-called classy bottles that cost twice as much.

 molten cakes with cherry sauce

 ravioli (from the can)

 patio/picnic, rock out

2005
Marques de Rojas
$9.99

Argentina

diego murillo

Have you seen those gas prices lately? It gives new meaning to "getting hosed." Though we try to use pedal power as often as possible, we also can't help feel the pinch—but mostly we have a similar gripe with wine. There was a time not long ago when it was easy to get a respectable $10 bottle. These days they're few and far between; wine inflation has even crept into these pages. So when there's a solid organic bottle for a tenner, we get giddy. Not the most complicated red, but good plum, caramel, herby, and smoky character at a nostalgic price.

 adobo

 teriyaki

 Wednesday wine

2005
Malbec
$9.99

la bastide

PRODUIT DE FRANCE
2005

LA BASTIDE

Vin de Pays de l'Herault

MIS EN BOUTEILLE
À LA PROPRIÉTÉ

13 % alc./vol.   750 ml

VIN ROUGE
RED WINE
PRODUCT OF FRANCE

If you're asking, "What's La Bastide?"

we're asking, "What rock have you been hiding under?" Since hitting local shelves a few years ago, La Bastide (formerly Domaine de la Bastide) is the king of the Ten Dolla Holla. Ask anyone: your hairdresser, the barista, whoever you're riding the elevator with. They've all got a case of La Bastide at home, and so should you. Raspberry and thyme unite for a medium-bodied wine fit for easygoing, heavy sipping.

 brie

 Wednesday wine, BYO

2005
Vin de Pays de l'Herault
$9.99

casal thaulero

Walking the $10 tightrope, Casal Thaulero's Sangiovese checks in as a contender for best value in 2008. Sure, all 100 bottles in this book are palate-bending, and redefining value, but there's something special about the $10 performers. Maybe it's because more often than not, we're in the liquor store with a tenner in our pockets. When this happens, we reach for the Casal Thaulero. Dense plum, sweet-smoky flavours, and just an amazing value from start to finish.

 loin

 burgers

 beginner

2005
Sangiovese
$9.99

finca flichman

We'll cut to the chase: overall this wine is quite "big" for a "cheap" bottle—the kind we love to put in this book. Its price tag belies the wine's character. This Malbec's got kick. It's smoky and juicy. Imagine smoking plum tobacco through a hookah. Back that up with a solid, full-bodied heft and great concentration, and Flichman has got a winner. Decant the bottle—or return to the leftovers the next day—and you'll find an even better wine after the rough edges have smoothed out.

MALBEC
OAK AGED
2006
WINE OF MENDOZA, ARGENTINA
RED WINE
PRODUCT OF ARGENTINA

2006
Malbec
$9.99

 apple wood smoked cheddar

 baba ghanouj

 BYO

South Africa

man vintners

We first tasted a MAN wine a few years back on a patio nestled in the hills of Stellenbosch in South African wine country. Revisiting this latest version of MAN's Shiraz, we're happy to report that this bottle still rocks the value quotient in a package that screams BYOB. Aside from the nice price, the wine looks the part of sophistication with a slick label and happening two-tone purple screw cap. Here's a crowd-pleasing red, redolent with sweet plum and soothing blackberry, a little spice and a hint of smoke, honest and impressively well-made.

 on its own

 BBQ-glazed ribs

 BYO, Wednesday wine

2005
Shiraz
$11.99

aliança

Possible uses for the name "Vista TR":

1. a Triumph convertible
2. the view from the Turkish Republic
3. Trent Reznor's record label
4. a scenic traffic rerouting
5. a panoramic tritium recovery plant
6. a Portuguese wine from the Tinta Roriz grape (plum and thyme aromas combine in this firm, medium-weight red wine that, unlike Nine Inch Nails and tritium, is very, very palatable)

 stew, stroganoff

 Wednesday wine, rock out

VISTA TR

2 0 0 3

TINTA RORIZ

**2003
Tinta Roriz
"Vista TR"
$11.99**

Australia

de bortoli

Petite Sirah, a.k.a. Durif, is a quirky grape. Often pronounced "indistinct" by the critics, Petite Sirah has nevertheless inspired a niche following among wine drinkers, the hardcore calling themselves "P.S.ers." The grape even has its own advocacy organization, "PSILY: P.S. I love you." After tasting this huge value dB, we're willing to sign on.

 tomme

 braised shank

 wine geek, winter warmer, cellar

2006
Petite Sirah
"dB"
$11.99

France

reserve de la perrière

We've got a sour taste on our palates from "reserve" wines, with their glossy connotation of superiority over the "non-reserve" swill. But there's no formal definition of "reserve" (except in a few countries, notably Spain). *Caveat emptor* is what we say. But for some reserve done right, pour some of the Reserve de la Perrière, an old world-ish rendition of strawberries, tilled earth, and dried herbs.

 leg

 burgers

 Wednesday wine, wine geek

2004
Fitou
$12.08

Australia

hardys

Not enough people write letters these days.

When was the last time you licked a stamp? If you can't recall, do yourself a favour. Pick up a bottle of this Stamp Series, pull out a pen and a pad of paper, pour yourself a glass, and scribe away. Heck, you can sprinkle a wine review in your epistle: soft plum, cherry, vanilla, ground black pepper. We guarantee that your handwritten note will make the day of the wine drinker on the receiving end.

 plum jam-glazed tenderloin

 roast veg sarnies

 beginner, patio/picnic

**2005
Shiraz/Cabernet Sauvignon
"Stamp Series"
$12.49**

bleasdale

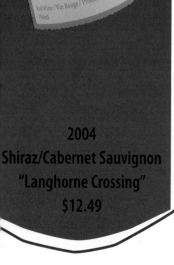

THE STORY OF
LANGHORNE
CROSSING
2004 SHIRAZ/CABERNET SAUVIGNON
LANGHORNE CREEK

THROUGHOUT THE
1840s ALFRED LANG-
HORNE DROVE HIS
CATTLE OVERLAND FROM VICTORIA
TO THE ADELAIDE MARKETS. ON
CROSSING THE AREA NOW KNOWN
AS LANGHORNE CREEK, HE RESTED
HIS WEARY HERD ON THE RICH,
FERTILE SURROUNDING FLOOD-
PLAINS. IN 1850, FRANK POTTS

ESTABLISHED BLEASDALE AND
HARNESSED THE NATURAL
OCCURRENCE OF THE FLOODS BY
DEVELOPING A UNIQUE FLOOD-
IRRIGATION SYSTEM TO WATER HIS
VINES. THIS SYSTEM IS STILL IN USE TODAY
PRODUCING
WINES OF
EXCELLENCE.   BLEASDALE

Red Wine / Vin Rouge / Product of Australia / Produit d'Australie
750ml

**2004
Shiraz/Cabernet Sauvignon
"Langhorne Crossing"
$12.49**

When the multi-tasking gets you down, simplify and take it back to the Good Life Triangle: good wine, good food, good people.

Crack open a bottle of Langhorne Crossing for an honest, quality red blend with all the juicy plum, strawberry pie, cracked black pepper, and hint of smoky oak a modern-day wine enthusiast desires. An easygoing wine without pretentiousness. Put down the BlackBerry and pick up the wine glass.

 hamburgers

 ratatouille

 Wednesday wine, BYO, patio/picnic

Argentina

bodega del fin del mundo

We've been to our share of wine regions, but never to el fin del mundo. Looks like they have grape vines there, and, if Southern Most is any indication, great wine. Straight from the end of the world comes this preternatural red oozing dense flavours of raspberries, cherries, and black forest cake. For dinner, sip it while contemplating, "Where exactly is the end of the world?"

 chops

 chicken enchiladas

 Wednesday wine, beginner

Merlot/Malbec/Cabernet Sauvignon "Southern Most" $12.95 2006

castillo de almansa

**2003
Reserva
$12.99**

Talk about halcyon times for capitalism.

Private equity is at all-time highs, with some signalling the death of public markets. The asset bubble has popped to the South, with all eyes turned to minute fluctuations of interest rates. We're all for Shumpetarian economics: bring on destructive capitalism, we say. Of course, we take comfort in knowing that we can invest in a case of $13 wine like this Almansa and while away the bear times with a surprisingly complex grab bag of old oak, plum, cigar, leather, and thyme—all in a reasonably rich, honest wine that works hard to please.

 manchego

 thyme-marinated chops

 wine geek, Wednesday wine

Argentina

pascual toso

Wine gets better with age. We thought the Pascual Toso was a pretty damn fine wine when we opened it—thick, heady, and reminiscent of coffee grinds and leather jackets. An hour later, gulping the last of the contents of the bottle, it was even better. Laced with character, the Toso is a serious drop of Malbec, oozing plum and tilled earth aromas all night long.

 burritos

 stew

 winter warmer, wine geek

2005
Malbec
$12.99

vitae

Wine is hott. (*Hott* being hotter than hot.) When the boyfriends start drinking it, when the DJ is drinking it, when the indie band drinks it, when someone's tagged the dumpster in your alley with their tasting notes, you know wine has saturated popular culture. This Sangiovese (Sangio, yo) is hott, exuding forever-hip cherry and wood-smoke flavours that will please the whole club.

 spaghetti & meatballs

 wine geek

VITAE
SANGIOVESE
ITALIA

PUGLIA
INDICAZIONE

2004
Sangiovese
$13.25

Spain

torres

If wines could rock, the Coronas would have long hair and high tops. Like the look, this wine dropped off the radar for a few years, but now it's back, rocking it, and taking names. Gone are the long, lonely days of emo, post-rock, Russian hip-hop, and bad Tempranillo. Put on a pair of black Levis, press play on some Destroyer, and swirl this double-kick noseful of Bing cherries, old wine casks, and fresh herbs.

 roast

 manchego

 rock out

2003
Tempranillo
"Coronas"
$13.56

carmen

If we weren't writing about wine, we'd be producing beats, holed up in a studio, tweaking knobs and looping drum kicks, giving Madlib and Timbaland a run for the money track. But we wouldn't knock back Cristal or swing Dom. We'd sip Pinot to unleash the creative juices. Pinot Noir and frustrated artist go hand in hand—the winemaker toiling with the "heartbreak grape." Carmen's is dusty black cherry in a cigar box, spicy with soft tannins, electro-funk in the bottle with a soulful fade-out.

 unidon (eel rice bowl)

 aperitif, rock out

CARMEN

Pinot Noir

2005
Valle de Aconcagua

**2005
Pinot Noir
$13.95**

casillero del diablo

Carmenère is cowboy wine. The grape makes intense, deep, dark-coloured reds that jump out of the glass to lasso your palate. The Casillero del Diablo is a great place to start on your Carmenère round-up, thanks to its chocolate and blackberry aromas, and chewy, herby, and coffee grind flavours. Rustle up some of your wine pardners. There's a new grape in town.

 braised short ribs

 cave-aged Gruyère

 Wednesday wine, beginner

RESERVA

Casillero del Diablo

CARMENERE 2005

CHILE

CONCHA Y TORO

2005
Carmenère
$13.95

tarapaca

**2005
Cabernet Sauvignon/Shiraz
"La Cuesta"
$13.99**

Wine tasting notes applied to everyday things.

- **Toothpaste:** Translucent green colour. Aroma of mint, with a subtle minty complexity. Mint flavour, with some sweetness. Minty finish.

- **Coffee:** Black hue and opaque. Aroma reminiscent of roasted coffee beans. Full-bodied, perhaps a recent vintage Kenya or Sumatra.

- **Tarapaca:** Vivid ruby colour. Rich cassis and blackberry aromas with smoky coffee notes. Ripe, mellow fruit flavours and bold acidity make this a delightful drink.

 chili

 rack

 BYO, wine geek

Argentina

lo tengo

Buenos Aires is the Paris of South America.

Grand architecture, style in abundance, an amazing food and wine scene. Back on the BA streets last year, the city seemed poised for a modern renaissance: the blocks of Palermo were awash with funky local haberdasheries, and the patios tucked along the alleys of La Boca were rollicking with good cheer. Modern Argentine times call for a modern Malbec like Lo Tengo, with lots of ripe plum and black fruit backed by a smooth, suave finish.

 chocolate

 asado

 beginner, Wednesday wine

2005
Malbec
$13.99

doña paula

Doña Paula kills the value category again (and again and again) with its Los Cardos line. This time they zero in on our taste buds and our wallets with a two thumbs-up Syrah. For the price of a movie, you can get 750 millilitres of this Argentine wine, smelling like braised pork belly and plum compote. Ditch the popcorn and press play on this fantastic red.

 belly

 Gruyère

 winter warmer, beginner

2004
Syrah
"Los Cardos"
$14.50

garnacha de fuego

Everything about this wine screams over the top. Just look at the label: flames belong on muscle cars, not wine bottles. Check the name: "Grenache of Fire"!?! Taste the vino: powerful cherry and raspberry, and dusty bramble concluded by a spicy, grippy tannin kick. This is a vinous middle finger to anything conventional, and just the sort of wine that gets our engines revving and our tongues rolling. Garrrrrrr-na-cha!

 on its own

 kebabs

 wine geek, romance

**2005
Garnacha
Joven Calatayud
$14.99**

redbank

2004
Shiraz
"The Long Paddock"
14.99

The Long Paddock will do a dandy job of quenching your thirst.

Which is fitting, as the wine is named after the old Australian practice of driving cattle along "the long paddock," the shoulders of highways, during drought in search of feed. Thankfully, Redbank's Long Paddock red saves us the trouble of getting dusty. Put a bottle atop the table, and satiate your thirst with this lean and mean Shiraz filled with cherry, blackberry, mint, and, yes, even some earthiness. This elegant style goes dynamite with food, particularly—dare we say—with a nice cut of beef.

 beef burritos

 grilled sausage

 beginner, aperitif

Italy

talamonti

If grapes were fashion trends, Montepulciano would be grunge. Not the most sophisticated of reds, it tends to be somewhat unrefined. But heck, Seattle showed us that plaid lumberjack coats can be fashionable, and Talamonti has brought us a stylish, "Moda," Montepulciano. Loads of sweet plum, cherry, and dark chocolate in a rich but still balanced style make for a solid, intense yet introspective bottle. It's only a matter of time before both grunge and Montepulciano d'Abruzzo are rocking tables.

 veal cacciatore

 mushroom medley

 Wednesday wine, patio/picnic

2003
Montepulciano d'Abruzzo
"Moda"
$14.99

mad dogs and englishmen

The heavyweight champion of critter labels, the Mad Dog can take on any marsupial, flightless waterfowl, or large aquatic reptile. Though denying any relation to the British Bulldog, the MD&E body slams big blackberry fruit, smoke, and spice, putting it in a gustatory league of its own. The crowd goes wild.

 roast

 brisket

 rock out, BYO

2005
Monastrell/Shiraz/Cabernet
$14.99

France

du peloux

Du Peloux struts its Natura Viti Charter, a credo to make wine responsibly. Not a precept to follow the phases of the moon or to dance clockwise in a deer bladder full of hemp tea, but just to make wine without dropkicking Mother Nature with herbicides. The result is a wine that's both natural in its make-up and fits our image of a naturally tasty Côtes du Rhône. Not like the illustrious neighbouring Châteauneuf-du-Pape, not like the trendy Vaqueras, but just a straight-up, aromatic orange peel, thyme, and raspberry medium-bodied Côtes du Rhône.

 sausage and leek gratin

 fondue

 wine geek

2004
Côtes du Rhône
"Terres du Rhône"
$14.99

arrowleaf

Do you care about food miles? With all the hoopla about climate change, we see a time when it won't be economically feasible to ship heavy wine in heavy glass bottles halfway around the world (don't even get us started on bottled water). It just doesn't make sense on several levels. In this future, we'd happily bring our gallon jug down to the local vino depot for some fine B.C. Pinot Noir, like this fresh cherry cola and toasty oak ArrowLeaf—in order to avoid the carbon tax.

 duck breast

 halibut with morel sauce

 Wednesday wine, patio/picnic

**2004
Pinot Noir
$15.90**

elephant island

Possibly the best tasting room in the Okanagan belongs to Elephant Island. Smack on the Naramata Bench this fruit winery offers its complementary tasting either at the usual bar or al fresco on the patio. Secure a piece of shade, then sit back as the kind staff delivers the delicious samples to you. This Black Currant is a patio pleaser: smelling like black currants (not surprisingly) with a hint of bell peppers, it has a truly intriguing meatiness that made us think this wine is a meal on its own.

 steak fajitas

 on its own

 patio/picnic, rock out, wine geek

2006
Black Currant
$15.95

las rocas de san alejandro

Las Rocas doesn't beat around the bush. This in-your-face wine announces itself gregariously from the first sniff. Gobs of black cherry and strawberry pie aromas mingle with some fresh earth. It's an aggressive combination that should be met by an equally assertive meal and a confident gulp, followed by conversation on politics and/or religion.

 hamburgers

 Moroccan-spiced shank

 rock out, wine geek

**2004
Garnacha
$15.95**

ricossa

Barbera for the masses! If only Barbera was abundant so that the masses could enjoy it. One of the rarer grape varieties on the liquor store shelf, Barbera is no globalized Cabernet or Shiraz. Rather, it's unique to northwest Italy, where it flourishes beside truffles and Milano fashion. Here, Ricossa brings us big Barbera value, with loads of cherry highlighted by vanilla accents. It's well-structured with plenty of lip-smacking acidity. Bargain Barbera at its best.

 grilled Portobello mushrooms

 pot roast

 wine geek, Wednesday wine

**2004
Barbera d'Asti
$15.95**

gray monk

Gray Monk goes old school to crack the books on fine Pinot Noir. With a nod to the village flats of Burgundy, the Monk treats us to a supremely drinkable bottle of Okanagan olfactory bliss. We're suckers for the low-alcohol, ample acidity renditions of this grape, not just because we can squeeze the whole bottle into one sitting, but because it's just so darn food-friendly. Whether we're talking stew or salmon, this tart cherry/forest fern number does the trick.

 stew

 mushroom risotto

 patio/picnic, wine geek

2005
Pinot Noir
$16.49

Spain

glorioso

Here's a glorious representation of ye olde Rioja. Amid the growing jungle of the New Spain—the Monastrells, the Garnachas—it's become quite the endangered species in sub-$20 territory. Granted, the Glorioso isn't entirely geriatric with its juicy cherry chocolate that tells all those dried-out old-timer Riojas to get out of the fast lane. We just love to taste a modern-minded Rioja that still stays true to its region.

 roast duck

 ribs

 romance, winter warmer

2003
Rioja
$16.99

wolf blass

Behold wine bottles gone wild. Taking on the Tetra Paks for most scandalous packaging, the Bilyara Reserve flaunts some pretty risqué plastic. The wine comes decked in a shatter-proof PET bottle—no different from bottled water or pop. To test it, we dropped a guy's bottle on the floor, and sure enough, no breakage. Note: it didn't help much in the ensuing bar fight. But where the Bilyara beats the boxes is in flavour. No flimsy wine here. This Cab is a solid mix of mint, black currants, and cocoa.

**2004
Cabernet Sauvignon
"Bilyara Reserve"
$16.99**

 T-bone

 on its own

 beginner

Italy

toscolo

Bonus points for the neon peach label. This wine screams New Rave, and hopefully this time around we'll ditch the Glow Sticks for a bottle of Toscolo. Toss on the Klaxons and pop the cork. Inside is a red wine with guts, classic black cherry, and cigar, with a fresh finish. This Chianti-lite oozes character and epitomizes the style of nicely balanced, food-versatile vino that we dig.

 falafel

 scaloppini

 rock out, beginner

2005
Chianti
$16.99

thorn-clarke

A benchmark blend.

Thorn-Clarke's Barossa Cuvée is a prime example of why we should drink grape goulash and quit getting hung up on solo Shirazes and Cabernets. A Dionysian party of grape varieties, this cuvée mingles the blackberry of Cabernet with the chocolate of Shiraz, plus the richness of Mourvèdre. The result is a kick-you-in-the-chops bottle of Barossa brilliance.

 chops

 BYO, winter warmer

**2003
Shiraz /Cabernet
Sauvignon/Mourvèdre
Terra Barossa
"Barossa Cuvée"
$17.99**

parducci

Stop the presses: there are two Petite Sirahs in this book! As Don Henley sang, "This is the end of the innocence." It's time to get juicy and lush, feather our hair, and bust a move with this ripe plum and herby style—a vibrant wine that shows sweet fruit but finishes bold and dry. "Just lay your head back on the ground / And let your hair fall all around me." P.S., we love you (page 95).

 stew

 pecorino pepato

 patio/picnic, rock out

**2004
Petite Sirah
$17.99**

altos de la hoya

Our favourite superhero was always Wolverine.

If Logan was a wine drinker—we only ever read about him using his adamantanium claws to "snik" open cans of beer—he'd drink something like the Altos de la Hoya. A gutsy 90% Monastrell/10% Grenache blend from the Spanish flats of Jumilla, La Hoya is big and brawny, with lots of black olive, savoury herb, and plum aromas followed by juicy plum and blackberry on the palate. It may not save the planet, but it's doing its part to rid the world of bad wine.

 grilled T-bone

 aged cheddar

 wine geek, BYO

2005
Jumilla
$17.99

Uruguay

pisano

Be the first on the block with a bottle of Tannat. A great way to expand your wine drinking into new territory, the Tannat grape is starting to make a name for itself in Uruguay, and we're happy at last to see an example on our shelves. The Pisano is one bold and concentrated bottle, with toasty mocha, oak, spicy plum, and currant—strong flavours that call out to be matched by Uruguay's rich and tasty asado roasts.

 porterhouse steak

 grilled leg

 wine geek

2005
Tannat
$18.95

carm

Bigger, riper, more oak.

This is the demise of red wine as we know it. Huge fruit and sweet toasty wood are getting jammed into our reds where there's no body to back it up. They talk big but can't deliver. They smell nice, but it's dull sipping. Not the Carm. The Carm is super-rich, with loads of smoke, leather and cigar, fresh mulberries, and chocolate-covered cherries. It has impeccable balance with just the right amount of tannin. This wine delivers.

 steak sandwich

 kebabs

 wine geek, winter warmer

DOURO
CARM
2004

2004
Douro
$19.75

Australia

the black chook

We like the wines, the wines that go boom. The Black Chook is the liquid version of the classic L'Trimm drum anthem—cranked out of a pair of 50-inch speakers, of course. The '80s Miami bass hip hop duo spared no expense in delivering the low frequency goods, mixed with a little turntable action, for a lovable track that we still can't take off "replay." This Chook struts a meaty, jammy Shiraz cut with a splash of Viognier for a floral, ginger root accent. Lots of boom, with a little trim.

 BBQ sirloin

 pepper-crusted lamb

 winter warmer, rock out

2006
Shiraz/Viognier
$19.95

saxenburg

Anyone with a bird phobia, look away.

Remember Hitchcock's *The Birds*? We can't. It keeps us up at night. With a life-sized picture of a bird feather on the label, don't pop a bottle of Saxenburg's Guinea Fowl on the table if there are any ornithophobiacs over for dinner. Instead, decant the wine, which is probably good for it anyway. Aromas of cherry pits and leather jackets emerge with some air, and, trust us, it tastes even better than that.

 coq au vin

 shank

 BYO

2003
Guinea Fowl
$19.95

Chile

montes

Cabernet Sauvignon has a patch over its eye, a gun, and a peg leg.

Carmenère has a sword, black tights, and nunchuks. They're both ready for action. Cabernet Sauvignon says "Arrr" and fires lead shot. Carmenère does a back flip and disappears. Cabernet Sauvignon rocks out. Carmenère strikes a pose. Cabernet Sauvignon brings big blackberry fruit and moderate tannins. Carmenère is damson plums and back bacon.

 sirloin

 shanks

 rock out, winter warmer

**2005
Cabernet Sauvignon/
Carmenère
$19.95**

croix du mayne

Cahors is the French appellation where wine is made from the Malbec grape. But in Cahors the grape is called Cot. Sounds like something you sleep on. No wonder the rest of the world goes for Malbec. Now that's a serious wine-sounding name. Cot or not, the Croix du Mayne is a beauty of a wine—plums, smoke, and spice—a bottle you definitely don't want to sleep on.

 baseball steak, meatballs

 wine geek, romance

**2004
Cahors
$19.95**

Chile

baron philippe de rothschild

"Second labels" are the affordable offspring of the illustrious and oft over-priced icons. We're big on third labels. Chateau Mouton Rothschild ($275) makes a second label, Le Petit Mouton ($70), which doesn't qualify for this book. Mouton Rothschild's venture into Chile called Escudo Rojo, however, does pass the test. This wine is a gorgeous mélange of raspberry, plum, cassis, and pencil shavings. Absolutely a candidate for your decanter: a few swirls will mellow out the wine's earthiness and leave you with a juicy, lip-smacking ride.

 baron

 wine geek, cellar

2003
Escudo Rojo
$19.95

ruffino

Carry your small dog in one purse. In the other, carry a bottle of Il Ducale. Both are equally fashionable, but only one tastes really good. Ruffino drops a chic wine into this bottle, straight out of classic Toscana, but without a hint of some fossilized cherry juice Chianti. Serious Tuscany and serious taste. Il Ducale is a stylish expression of raspberries, plums, and cherry compote. With its earthy complexity backed by some sweet cocoa action and brilliant acidity, you can BYO this to any downtown party.

 veal cutlets

 Saint-Nectaire

 BYO, romance

RUFFINO

IL DUCALE

2003

**2003
Toscana
"Il Ducale"
$19.99**

Australia

angus

The Angus is like a movie that tugs all the right strings, at the right times. It isn't quirky like Scorsese's *King of Comedy* or perpetually disturbing like Herzog's *Grizzly Man* (both great flicks) but rather this Aussie ambrosia guides you through a gastronomic odyssey, all the while giving you exactly what you want before you even know it—butterscotch, bacon, and blackberry rolled into one. You dream about this hedonistic mishmash, but only after sipping the Angus do you realize it can be beautiful.

 Angus-certified

 on its own

 BYO

angus
THE BULL

Cabernet Sauvignon
Vintage 2005

Wine of Australia
750 mL

2005
Cabernet Sauvignon
$19.99

santa rita

**2003
Cabernet Sauvignon
"Medalla Real"
$19.99**

**Behold, a Cab Sauv
with both power and
panache.** We taste a lot of
Cabernets with power—big uppercutting,
headbutting, leg-wrestling Cabernets
great for some K-1 action, but not so great
when we don't feel like stepping into the
ring with our evening's beverage choice.
And we taste a lot of Cabernets with
panache, but panache alone won't get you
far. Santa Rita matches the two perfectly
in this bottle of Medalla Real—a load of
ripe blackberry and sweet oak checked by
lithesome cassis and solid tannins.

 Salisbury steak

 Comté

 winter warmer

Italy

viberti

Wine advice is weird.

Once, a colleague advised us to buy
bottles if they had a picture of the
winemaker on the label like a stamp
of guarantee. They reasoned that the
winemaker wouldn't dare put his likeness
on a sub-par product. Perhaps, but we've
also had a lot of good wines with labels
depicting châteaux, vineyards, even the
occasional animal. But what to make of a
wine slapped with a sticker depicting the
winemaker bathing in a tub of grapes?
This Nebbiolo is a solid, structured drop
packed with black cherry and backed by
a savoury spice.

 pasta with wild mushrooms

 wine geek, winter warmer

2004
Nebbiolo
Langhe
$19.99

sumac ridge

On our MySpace profiles, we list a fondness for Cabernet Franc, not typically a crowd pleaser. And in today's connected, long-tail economy world, we hope that Cab Franc's niche will grow. Hopefully the wisdom of the crowd will take over. Cabernet Franc is awkward in an endearing way. Leafy, pencil shavings, earthy—these are Franc's unique personality traits.

 chèvre

 sausage with mint

 wine geek, cellar

**2005
Cabernet Franc
"Black Sage Vineyard"
$19.99**

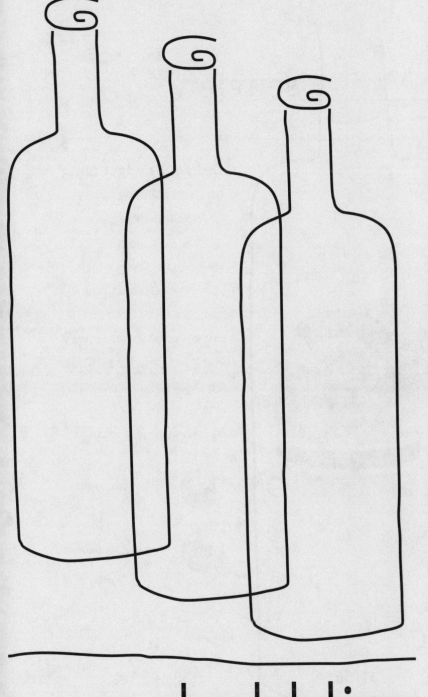

the bubblies

seaview

Get your budget bling on. Nothing says "keeping it real" like a bottle of bubbly. And nothing says "holla" like Seaview's Brut. This is a tasty, economically minded bub that lets everyone—including struggling rap artists—get their sip on. Sparkling socialism? No, we'll always have Dom to separate the P. Diddys from us P. Ons. But after a few glasses of Seaview, we'll swear that we can spit out a rhyme better than that Combs guy.

 Sunday brunch omelet

 romance, Wednesday wine

Brut

$13.56

France

veuve du vernay

Yeah, we drink Veuve.

If someone else is buying we'll happily drink that orange-labelled Cliquot stuff seven days a week, otherwise we'll reach for the "other" Veuve. Veuve du Vernay has long been recognized as a classic bargain bubbly, and this Blanc de Blancs is a straight-up crowd pleaser showing grapefruit and a soft mousse that will pimp out your mimosa or handle its own sipped neat.

 on its own

 practically any

 aperitif, BYO

Brut
"Blanc de Blancs"
$13.99

deinhard

**Riesling Sekt
"Lila"
$14.99**

The world's greatest grilled cheese sandwich is found in London's Borough Market. At least it used to be. Just a guy with a panini press, top-notch sourdough, some grilled onions, and mounds of cheddar. Nothing complicated, served in a plain paper napkin to be eaten on the spot. Anyway, when we cracked open this bottle of Lila, all we could think about was tucking into one of those cheese-tastic sandwiches and sipping this killer-value bubbly in between bites. Comfort food, and a perfect pairing.

 grilled

 on its own

 BYO, Wednesday wine

codorníu

Booyah big bubbles in your face! We like our bubbly both ways, sometimes with the finesse of a fine mousse, other times bursting with a bead of exuberant fizz. The style depends on the grapes in the bottle and the method used to get the bubbles. This 100% Pinot Noir Cava falls in the latter camp and works it well thanks to the rich, fuller style imparted from the red grapes.

 mussels with chorizo

 chicken tamales

 wine geek, romance

Pinot Noir Cava
$19.99

monmousseau

Bubble: to celebrate life's accomplishments and to plan life's grand schemes. There's no shortage of occasions for bubble, which is why we default to non-Champagne sparkling wine. If we drank Champagne for each of these occasions, we'd be broke. To keep things fizzy and French, we opt for this Monmousseau from the Loire that works hard to please with its fun and fruity nature—a sparkling wine style that's a crowd pleaser, and pairing well with life's multitude of occasions.

 on its own

 green curry

 you need more?

2000
"Cuvée J.M. Brut"
$19.99

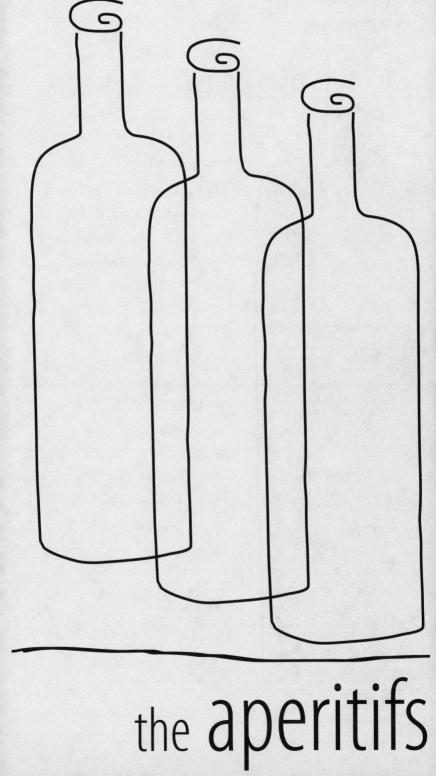

the aperitifs

cinzano

The aperitif is the ultimate patio accessory. And Cinzano is a classic. Sadly, aperitifs aren't getting much love these days. We concur with the late Spanish filmmaker Luis Buñuel, who wrote, "The decline of the aperitif may well be one of the most depressing phenomena of our time." Pour it easy over ice, add a slice of lemon, and you're golden. It's available in a variety of flavours, but we default to the real deal Rosso, with a sweet orange zest and savory aromatic allure that offers a nice contrast to the inherent bite of the herbs and spices. If you embrace patio lounging or outdoor living rooms, toss a bottle of Cinzano in your bar.

 on its own

 patio/picnic, BYOB

"Rosso"
$11.75 (for 1 litre)

gonzalez byass

Tio Pepe made an appearance in the first edition of *Had a Glass*.

It's here again because it's a) still amazingly tasty and b) a dollar cheaper. Besides, a good sherry is like a good suit—when made well, they're both timelessly stylish. Sherry styles are not meant to change from year to year. Instead, different vintages are blended together to create one consistent style. To learn more, look up *solera* on Wikipedia. Here, good ol' Uncle Pepe maintains the classic nutty, briny, lip-smackingly dry qualities that showcase a hallmark fino—an appeal that wears well through the years.

 pan-toasted almonds

 on its own

 picnic, aperitif

Fino Sherry
"Tio Pepe"
$18.99

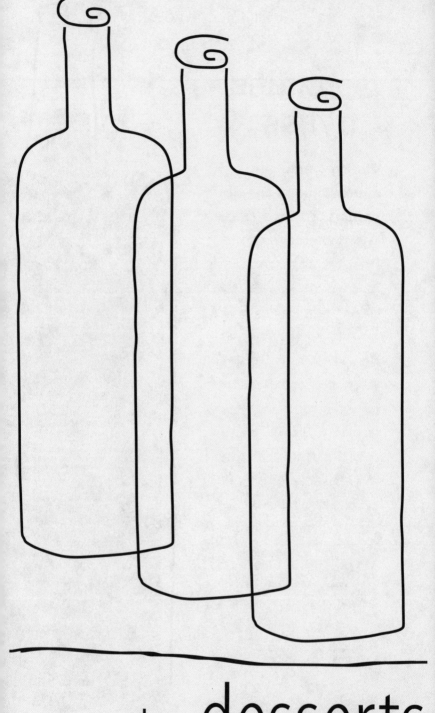

the desserts

cantine pellegrino

We'd like to explain something about goal-setting and Marsala.

Goal-setting is worthwhile and important for getting things done. Like writing wine reviews. Marsala is also worthwhile—the sweet, nutty, caramel-smelling elixir, silky and delicious like no other fortified beverage. It isn't the vodka and Red Bull Slurpee of the just-turned-19-year-old kid next door. Yuck. Anyway, we set goals for ourselves and sip Marsala.

 on its own

 winter warmer

Marsala Superiore "Garibaldi Dolce" $13.99 (for 375 mL)

lustau

**Deluxe Cream
Sherry
"Reserva Superior
Capataz Andrés"
$13.99 (for 375 mL)**

Goodness gracious, this is one sweet wine.

And although we do literally mean sweet, we're more emphatically talking sweeeeet—that term that too many of our friends developed as a linguistic tick about a decade ago. Thankfully, sweet has gone the way of phat, bad (meaning good), and, to a lesser extent, awesome. We're left with a gorgeous bottle that represents pure raisiny hedonism, as in plump golden Thompsons oozing out of the glass and licking your tongue. A true sipping wine, the ultra-luscious Lustau Cream will rock the end of your night, either on its own or atop some vanilla ice cream.

 on its own

 romance, wine geek

fonseca

Highly drinkable.

Redefining the "sticky," Fonseca's LBV is not sweet but a mouthful of plums and thyme, backed by shades of tobacco leaf and cigar smoke. There's a serious, savoury edge to this port, separating it from any stereotypical tooth-rattling syrup, and prompting us to pour a second glass. Break out a block of cheese and some fresh fruit, and we'll be pouring a third.

 fresh fruits & nuts

 blue

 romance, winter warmer

2000
Port
"Late Bottled Vintage"
$16.49 (for 375 mL)

yalumba

**Tawny Port
"Clocktower"
$19.07**

Tawny is just one of those words that's fun to say. And Tawny's just one of those ports that's fun to drink. Especially when it's as good as Clocktower. There are four basic types of Port. Vintage is top dog. Then we have late-bottled vintage (LBV), Tawny, and finally Ruby. What makes a Tawny? More time in oak barrels, which turns the fortified wine its namesake, a wonderful amber colour. What's in a Tawny? Well, this bottle highlights classic orange peel and caramel, almond skin and toffee, a wicked combination to end the meal.

 on its own

 fondue

 Wednesday wine

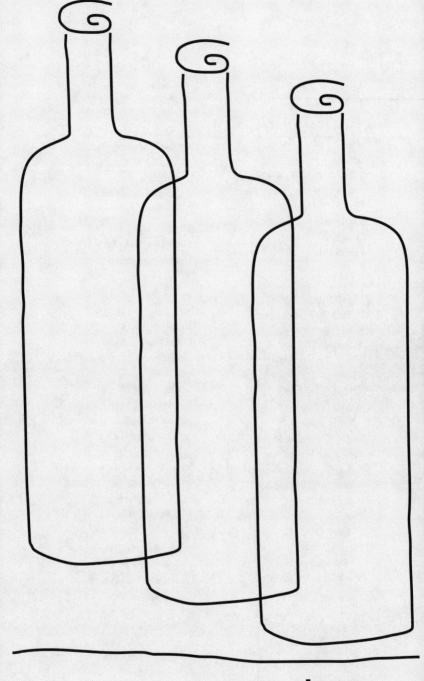

the indices

wines by country

Argentina

Bodega Del Fin Del Mundo Merlot/
    Malbec/Cabernet "Southern Most" 99
Diego Murillo Malbec 89
Dõna Paula Syrah "Los Cardos" 108
Finca Flichman Malbec 92
Lo Tengo Malbec 107
Pascual Toso Malbec 101

Australia

Angus Cabernet Sauvignon 133
The Black Chook Shiraz Viognier 127
Bleasdale Shiraz/Cabernet Sauvignon
    "Langhorne Crossing" 98
De Bortoli Petite Sirah "dB" 95
Grant Burge Semillon/Sauvignon Blanc
    "Barossa Vines" 70
Hardys Shiraz/Cabernet Sauvignon
    "Stamp Series" 97
Heartland "Stickleback White" 57
McWilliam's Riesling 61
Penfolds Chardonnay "Koonunga Hill" 59
Redbank Shiraz "The Long Paddock" 110
Seaview Brut 138
Thorn-Clarke Shiraz/Cab/Mourvèdre
    "Barossa Cuvée" 122
Wolf Blass Cabernet Sauvignon
    "Bilyara Reserve" 120
Yalumba Tawny Port "Clocktower" 150

Austria

Schloss Gobelsburg Grüner Veltliner
    "Gobelsburger" 79

British Columbia

Arrowleaf Pinot Noir 114
Elephant Island Black Currant 115
Gray Monk Pinot Noir 118

Inniskillin Chenin Blanc
    "Discovery Series" 65
Mission Hill Pinot Grigio
    "Five Vineyards" 64
Quails' Gate Rosé 85
Red Rooster Gewürztraminer
    "Reserve" 75
See Ya Later Ranch Chardonnay 80
Sumac Ridge Cabernet Franc 136
Wild Goose Riesling 63

California

Bonterra Chardonnay 71
Parducci Petite Sirah 123
Wente Chardonnay 67

Chile

Adobe Chardonnay 54
Anakena Viognier 66
Carmen Pinot Noir 104
Casillero del Diablo Carmenère 105
Cono Sur Gewürztraminer 49
Montes Cabernet Sauvignon/
    Carmenère 129
Rothschild Escudo Rojo 131
Santa Rita Cabernet Sauvignon
    "Medalla Real" 134
Santa Rita Sauvignon Blanc "120" 51
Tarapaca Cabernet/Shiraz "La Cuesta" 106
Tarapaca Sauvignon Blanc 47
Viña Chocalán Rosé Syrah/Petit Verdot 83

France

André Lurton Château Bonnet
    "Entre-Deux-Mers" 69
Chapoutier Côteaux du Tricastin
    "La Ciboise" 58
Château de Chasseloir Muscadet Sevre et
    Maine Sur Lie 76
Croix du Mayne Cahors 130
Du Peloux Côtes-du-Rhône
    "Terres du Rhône" 113
La Bastide 90

Laroche Viognier 53
Lurton Sauvignon Blanc
    "Les Fumées Blanches" 52
Monmousseau "Cuvée J.M. Brut" 142
Veuve du Vernay Brut
    "Blanc de Blancs" 139
Reserve de la Perrière Fitou 96

Germany
Deinhard Riesling Sekt "Lila" 140
Leitz Riesling 78
Lingenfelder Riesling "Bird Label" 72
Rudolf Müller Riesling/Chardonnay 50

Hungary
Dunavar Pinot Gris 46

Italy
Bollini Pinot Grigio 74
Cantine Pellegrino Marsala Superiore
    "Garibaldi Dolce" 147
Casal Thaulero Sangiovese 91
Cinzano "Rosso" 144
Feudo Arancio Grillo Sicilia 62
Frescobaldi Pomino Bianco 77
MandraRossa Chardonnay 55
Ricossa Barbera d'Asti 117
Ruffino "Il Ducale" 132
Talamonti Montepulciano d'Abruzzo
    "Moda" 111
Toscolo Chianti 121
Viberti Nebbiolo 135
Villa Teresa Pinot Grigio 56
Vitae Sangiovese 102

New Zealand
Babich Sauvignon Blanc 68
Jackson Sauvignon Blanc 81
Villa Maria Sauvignon Blanc 73

Portugal
Aliança Tinta Roriz "Vista TR" 94
Carm Douro 126
Fonseca Port "Late Bottled Vintage" 149
Gazela Vinho Verde 48

South Africa
MAN Vintners Shiraz 93
Saxenburg "Guinea Fowl" 123

Spain
Altos de la Hoya Monastrell 124
Bodegas Piqueras Marques de Rojas 88
Castillo de Almansa Reserva 100
Codorníu Pinot Noir Cava 141
Garnacha de Fuego "Old Vines" 109
Glorioso Crianza Rioja 119
Las Rocas de San Alejandro Garnacha 116
Lustau Deluxe Cream "Reserva Superior
    Capataz Andrés" 148
Mad Dogs and Englishmen Monastrell/
    Shiraz/Cabernet 112
Marqués de Cáceres Rosado 84
Tio Pepe Fino Sherry 145
Torres Tempranillo "Coronas" 103

Uruguay
Pisano Tannat 125

Washington
Chateau Ste. Michelle Riesling 60

wines by type

Barbera
Ricossa Barbera d'Asti 117

Cabernet Franc
Sumac Ridge Cabernet Franc 136

Cabernet Sauvignon
Angus Cabernet Sauvignon 133
Santa Rita Cabernet Sauvignon
"Medalla Real" 133
Wolf Blass Cabernet Sauvignon
"Bilyara Reserve" 120

Carmenère
Casillero del Diablo Carmenère 105

Chardonnay
Adobe Chardonnay 54
Bonterra Chardonnay 71
MandraRossa Chardonnay 55
Penfolds Chardonnay "Koonunga Hill" 59
See Ya Later Ranch Chardonnay 80
Wente Chardonnay 67

Chenin Blanc
Inniskillin Chenin Blanc
"Discovery Series" 65

Fortified
Cantine Pellegrino Marsala Superiore
"Garibaldi Dolce" 147
Cinzano "Rosso" 144
Fonseca Port "Late Bottled Vintage" 149
Lustau Deluxe Cream "Reserva Superior
Capataz Andrés" 148
Tio Pepe Fino Sherry 145
Yalumba Tawny Port "Clocktower" 150

Fruit
Elephant Island Black Currant 115

Garnacha/Grenache
Garnacha de Fuego "Old Vines" 109
Las Rocas de San Alejandro Garnacha 116

Gewürztraminer
Cono Sur Gewürztraminer 49
Red Rooster Gewürztraminer
"Reserve" 75

Grillo
Feudo Arancio Grillo Sicilia 62

Grüner Veltliner
Schloss Gobelsburg Grüner Veltliner
"Gobelsburger" 79

Malbec
Croix du Mayne Cahors 130
Diego Murillo Malbec 89
Finca Flichman Malbec 92
Lo Tengo Malbec 107
Pascual Toso Malbec 101

Monastrell
Altos de la Hoya Monastrell 124

Montepulciano
Citra Montepulciano d'Abruzzo 87
Talamonti Montepulciano d'Abruzzo
"Moda" 111

Muscadet
Château de Chasseloir Muscadet Sevre et
Maine Sur Lie 76

Nebbiolo
Viberti Nebbiolo 135

Petite Sirah
De Bortoli Petite Sirah "dB" 95
Parducci Petite Sirah 123

Pinot Grigio/Pinot Gris
Bollini Pinot Grigio 74
Dunavar Pinot Gris 46
Mission Hill Pinot Grigio
"Five Vineyards" 64
Villa Teresa Pinot Grigio 56

Pinot Noir

Arrowleaf Pinot Noir 114
Carmen Pinot Noir 104
Gray Monk Pinot Noir 118

Red Blend

Aliança Tinta Roriz "Vista TR" 94
Bleasdale Shiraz/Cabernet Sauvignon
"Langhorne Crossing" 98
Bodega Del Fin Del Mundo Merlot/
Malbec/Cabernet "Southern Most" 99
Bodegas Piqueras Marques de Rojas 88
Castillo de Almansa Reserva 100
Carm Douro 126
Du Peloux Côtes-du-Rhône
"Terres du Rhône" 113
Hardys Shiraz/Cabernet Sauvignon
"Stamp Series" 97
La Bastide 90
Mad Dogs and Englishmen Monastrell/
Shiraz/Cabernet 112
Montes Cabernet Sauvignon/
Carmenère 129
Redbank Shiraz "The Long Paddock" 110
Reserve de la Perrière Fitou 96
Ruffino "Il Ducale" 132
Rothschild Escudo Rojo 131
Saxenburg "Guinea Fowl" 128
Thorn-Clarke Shiraz/Cab/Mourvèdre
"Barossa Cuvée" 122

Riesling

Chateau Ste. Michelle Riesling 60
Leitz Riesling 78
Lingenfelder Riesling "Bird Label" 72
McWilliam's Riesling 61
Wild Goose Riesling 63

Rosé

Marqués de Cáceres Rosado 84
Quails' Gate Rosé 85
Viña Chocalán Rosé Syrah/Petit Verdot 83

Sangiovese

Casal Thaulero Sangiovese 91

Toscolo Chianti 121
Vitae Sangiovese 102

Sauvignon Blanc

Babich Sauvignon Blanc 68
Lurton Sauvignon Blanc
"Les Fumées Blanches" 52
Jackson Sauvignon Blanc 81
Santa Rita Sauvignon Blanc "120" 51
Tarapaca Sauvignon Blanc 47
Villa Maria Sauvignon Blanc 73

Shiraz/Syrah

The Black Chook Shiraz Viognier 127
Dõna Paula Syrah "Los Cardos" 108
MAN Vintners Shiraz 93

Sparkling

Codorníu Pinot Noir Cava 141
Deinhard Riesling Sekt "Lila" 140
Monmousseau "Cuvée J.M. Brut" 142
Seaview Brut 138
Veuve du Vernay Brut
"Blanc de Blancs" 139

Tannat

Pisano Tannat 125

Tempranillo

Glorioso Crianza Rioja 119
Torres Tempranillo "Coronas" 103

Viognier

Anakena Viognier 66
Laroche Viognier 53

White Blend

André Lurton Château Bonnet
"Entre-Deux-Mers" 69
Chapoutier Côteaux du Tricastin
"La Ciboise" 58
Frescobaldi Pomino Bianco 77
Gazela Vinho Verde
Grant Burge Semillon/Sauvignon Blanc
"Barossa Vines" 70
Heartland "Stickleback White" 57
Rudolf Müller Riesling/Chardonnay 50

wines by food

Beef

Aliança Tinta Roriz "Vista TR" 94
Altos de la Hoya Monastrell 124
Angus Cabernet Sauvignon 133
The Black Chook Shiraz/Viognier 127
Bleasdale Shiraz/Cabernet Sauvignon
    "Langhorne Crossing" 98
Bodegas Piqueras Marques de Rojas 88
Carm Douro 126
Casal Thaulero Sangiovese 91
Casillero del Diablo Carmenère 105
Croix du Mayne Cahors 130
Gray Monk Pinot Noir 118
La Bastide 90
Las Rocas de San Alejandro Garnacha 116
Lo Tengo Malbec 107
Mad Dogs and Englishmen Monastrell/
    Shiraz/Cabernet 112
MAN Vintners Shiraz 93
Montes Cabernet Sauvignon/
    Carmenère 129
Parducci Petite Sirah 123
Pascual Toso Malbec 101
Pisano Tannat 125
Reserve de la Perrière Fitou 96
Ricossa Barbera d'Asti 117
Rothschild Escudo Rojo 131
Ruffino "Il Ducale" 132
Santa Rita Cabernet Sauvignon
    "Medalla Real" 134
Talamonti Montepulciano d'Abruzzo
    "Moda" 111
Tarapaca Cabernet Sauvignon/Shiraz
    "La Cuesta" 106
Torres Tempranillo "Coronas" 103
Vitae Sangiovese 102

Wolf Blass Cabernet Sauvignon
    "Bilyara Reserve" 120

Cheese

Altos de la Hoya Monastrell 124
André Lurton Château Bonnet
    "Entre-Deux-Mers" 69
Cantine Pellegrino Marsala Superiore
    "Garibaldi Dolce" 147
Casillero del Diablo Carmenère 105
Castillo de Almansa Reserva 100
Citra Montepulciano d'Abruzzo 87
De Bortoli Petite Sirah "dB" 95
Deinhard Riesling Sekt "Lila" 140
Doña Paula Syrah "Los Cardos" 108
Dunavar Pinot Gris 46
Fonseca Port "Late Bottled Vintage" 149
Inniskillin Chenin Blanc
    "Discovery Series" 65
La Bastide 90
Marques de Cáceres Rosado 84
Monmousseau "Cuvée J.M. Brut" 142
Parducci Petite Sirah 123
Penfolds Chardonnay "Koonunga Hill" 59
Ruffino "Il Ducale" 132
Santa Rita Cabernet Sauvignon
    "Medalla Real" 134
Schloss Gobelsburg Grüner Veltliner
    "Gobelsburger" 79
Sumac Ridge Cabernet Franc 136
Torres Tempranillo "Coronas" 103

Chocolate

Bodegas Piqueras Marques de Rojas 88
Elephant Island Black Currant 115
Lo Tengo Malbec 107

Fish

Anakena Viognier 66
Arrowleaf Pinot Noir 114
Carmen Pinot Noir 104
Frescobaldi Pomino Bianco 77
Jackson Sauvignon Blanc 81

Lurton Sauvignon Blanc
"Les Fumées Blanches" 52
Rudolf Müller Riesling/Chardonnay 50
Tarapaca Sauvignon Blanc 47
Wild Goose Riesling 63

Lamb

Carm Douro 126
Castillo de Almansa Reserva 100
De Bortoli Petite Sirah "dB" 95
Las Rocas de San Alejandro Garnacha 116
Mad Dogs and Englishmen Monastrell/
Shiraz/Cabernet 112
Montes Cabernet Sauvignon/
Carmenère 129
Pascual Toso Malbec 101
Pisano Tannat 125
Reserve de la Perrière Fitou 96
Saxenburg "Guinea Fowl" 128
Sumac Ridge Cabernet Franc 136
Tarapaca Shiraz "La Cuesta" 106
Thorn-Clarke "Barossa Cuvée" 122

On Its Own

Angus Cabernet Sauvignon 133
Bollini Pinot Grigio 74
Cantine Pellegrino Marsala Superiore
"Garibaldi Dolce" 147
Chateau Ste. Michelle Riesling 60
Cinzano Rosso 144
Deinhard Riesling Sekt "Lila" 140
Elephant Island Black Currant 115
Gazela Vinho Verde 48
Lo Tengo Malbec 107
MandraRossa Chardonnay 55
MAN Vintners Shiraz 93
Monmousseau "Cuvée J.M. Brut" 142
Quails' Gate Rosé 85
Santa Rita Sauvignon Blanc "120" 51
Seaview Brut 138
See Ya Later Ranch Chardonnay 80
Wolf Blass Cabernet Sauvignon
"Bilyara Reserve" 120

Pork

Bodega Del Fin Del Mundo Merlot/
Malbec "Southern Most" 99
Casal Thaulero Sangiovese 91
Chateau Ste. Michelle Riesling 60
Cono Sur Gewürztraminer 49
Doña Paula Syrah "Los Cardos" 108
Du Peloux Côtes-du-Rhône
"Terres du Rhône" 113
Glorioso Crianza Rioja 119
Hardys Shiraz/Cabernet Sauvignon
"Stamp Series" 97
Inniskillin Chenin Blanc
"Discovery Series" 65
Jackson Sauvignon Blanc 81
Leitz Riesling 78
Lingenfelder Riesling "Bird Label" 72
Rothschild Escudo Rojo 131
Thorn-Clarke "Barossa Cuvée" 122
Toscolo Chianti 121
Wild Goose Riesling 63

Poultry

Adobe Chardonnay 54
Arrowleaf Pinot Noir 114
Bodega Del Fin Del Mundo Merlot/
Malbec/Cabernet "Southern Most" 99
Bollini Pinot Grigio 74
Bonterra Chardonnay 71
Carmen Pinot Noir 104
Chapoutier Côteaux du Tricastin
"La Ciboise" 58
Codorníu Pinot Noir Cava 141
Feudo Arancio Grillo Sicilia 62
Glorioso Rioja 119
Heartland Crianza "Stickleback White" 57
Laroche Viognier 53
Leitz Riesling 78
Penfolds Chardonnay "Koonunga Hill" 59
Red Rooster Gewürztraminer
"Reserve" 75
Santa Rita Sauvignon Blanc "120" 51

Saxenburg "Guinea Fowl" 128
Seaview Brut 138
Wente Chardonnay 67

Shellfish

Chapoutier Côteaux du Tricastin
"La Ciboise" 58
Château de Chasseloir Muscadet Sevre et
Maine Sur Lie 76
Codorníu Pinot Noir Cava 141
MandraRossa Chardonnay 55
McWilliam's Riesling 61
Quails' Gate Rosé 85
Schloss Gobelsburg Grüner Veltliner
"Gobelsburger" 79
See Ya Later Ranch Chardonnay 80
Tarapaca Sauvignon Blanc 47
Wente Chardonnay 67

Spicy

Anakena Viognier 66
Babich Sauvignon Blanc 68
The Black Chook Shiraz/Viognier 127
Heartland "Stickleback White" 57
Monmousseau "Cuvée J.M. Brut" 142
Rudolf Müller Riesling/Chardonnay 50

Vegetarian

Adobe Chardonnay 54.
André Lurton Château Bonnet
"Entre-Deux-Mers" 69
Babich Sauvignon Blanc 68
Bleasdale Shiraz/Cabernet Sauvignon
"Langhorne Crossing" 98
Bollini Pinot Grigio 74
Bonterra Chardonnay 71
Château de Chasseloir Muscadet Sevre et
Maine Sur Lie 76
Citra Montepulciano d'Abruzzo 87
Dunavar Pinot Gris 46
Feudo Arancio Grillo Sicilia 62
Fonseca Port "Late Bottled Vintage" 149
Frescobaldi Pomino Bianco 77
Grant Burge Semillon/Sauvignon Blanc
"Barossa Vines" 70
Gray Monk Pinot Noir 118
Hardys Shiraz/Cabernet Sauvignon
"Stamp Series" 97
Lurton Sauvignon Blanc
"Les Fumées Blanches" 52
Marques de Cáceres Rosado 84
McWilliam's Riesling 61
Ricossa Barbera d'Asti 117
Talamonti Montepulciano d'Abruzzo
"Moda" 111
Toscolo Chianti 121
Viberti Nebbiolo 135

acknowledgements

"Three times lucky," they say. But this third edition of *Had a Glass* would never have gone to press if left to the authors alone. We'd like to extend our gratitude to Robert and the hard-working staff at Whitecap for making this 2008 edition happen. A high-five to Ben, who meticulously edited the book, ensuring we stayed on the correct side of PC. And a shout-out to Jesse and Michelle, who dropped some great design upon these pages.

We're eternally—or at least annually—grateful to family and friends for providing invaluable support by relating their wine experiences, giving us feedback on our reviews, and (enthusiastically) offering their tasting expertise. A big hug to Mimi for yet another year of gastronomic support. We'd be lost without her culinary savvy. And special gratitude to Mai and Karen for their endless patience as we tried desperately to settle on the 100th wine.

We'd like to raise a glass to the agents and wineries that have supported us in this venture. We hope new and exciting wines continue to land on our shores and spring from your cellars—this is what makes wine drinking worthwhile. A kampai to the Vancouver wine media who acknowledge our cause and have supported us wholeheartedly. Special thanks goes to the *Province* for giving the "Wine Guys" a home, as well as *TASTE* magazine and every other publication that provides the oh-so important venues for spreading our wine love.